# Through A Feudal Window

INDRAJIT SINGH RATHORE

# Through A Feudal Window

## Chronicles of a Rajput Clan

New Age Books

New Delhi (India)

**THROUGH A FEUDAL WINDOW: Chronicles of a Rajput Clan**

*Published by*
**NEW AGE BOOKS**
A-44 Naraina Industrial Area, Phase-I
New Delhi (India)-110 028
E-mail: nab@newagebooksindia.com
Website: www.newagebooksindia.com

ISBN: 978-81-7822-466-4

First Edition: Delhi, **2014**



*Printed and published by*
RP Jain for New Age Books
A-44, Naraina Industrial Area
Phase-I, New Delhi-110 028. India

# Contents

***for***

*Dhruv and Neel*

H.H. GAJSINGH II
MAHARAJA OF MARWAR-JODHPUR

UMAID BHAWAN PALACE
JODHPUR - 342 006
**31st Dec., 2013**

## MESSAGE

**I am very pleased that Rao Indrajit Singh Rathore of Masuda has undertaken the project of writing his family-the Mertia Rathore' history. It is very important that history is revisited from time to time and examined with newer perspectives.**

**Dudaji from whom the Mertias sprung was son of my ancestor Rao Jodha who founded Jodhpur and built the Mehrangarh Fort in 1459. As 39th Rathore clan Chief I have always been very proud of my brothers, the Mertia Rathores , for their bravery and courage. I am reminded of a Sanskrit sloka from the Rig Veda, while thinking of Rao Indrajit Singhji' ancestors**

***Shauryam tejo dhritir dakshyam, yudde chapy - apalayanam,***

***Danam ishvara bhavashcha, kshtram karma savabhava jam***

**"Valour, brilliance, determination, skillfulness, steadfastness in battle,**

**Generosity and authority are natural qualities of work for keshatriya."**

These are the qualities that set the Rajput clans apart & has ensured their endurance and survival though the ages - they pre-dated the Moghuls & survived the British & still retain their identity in Republican India.

Mertia Rathore are a unique example - throughout their history consistently identified themselves with quality of valor ( Sanskrit: shauryam; Marwari: rajputai).

The Mertia Rathores were most feared on the battlefield over the centuries. My ancestors have depended heavily on them in certain times of war. In fact in 1889, the Jodhpur Lancer's 'A' Squadron was the Mertia Squadron.

GAJSINGH
MAHARAJA OF JODHPUR

# Acknowledgements

This book only became possible because in a sense my father willed it. He was always passionate about ancestry and succeeded in firing my own curiosity to learn more. At school my first noteworthy project was a brief sketch of ancestral history illustrated with miniatures, which won an award.

There was no dearth of information as our archives were meticulously maintained and preserved. My father had also undertaken to have important archival material bearing on the ancestors, painstakingly translated from the Rajasthani dialect into Hindi and English by earnest linguists. This eventually became the invaluable source material on which I have relied. Equally, anecdotes of events were frequently relayed by him at meals and times of leisure, filling our imagination with his colourful narrative. There was also the large collection of miniature paintings in our 'Jot Dans' which proved to have unique value allowing rare visualization of personalities and their pursuits from the mysterious past.

While the Estate had yet to be abolished after independence, the staff lingered on. One of the retinue included a 'Charan', royal bard, by the name of Gunidanji. His other worldly demeanour, hypnotic red eyes and sonorous voice often related stories through couplets and resounding ballads from our historical past, with gusto and passion.

With all these influences and incitements it was only a matter of time before the childhood project metamorphosed into a dedicated undertaking to write a mature history of the clan which emerged finally in the form of this book, '*Through A Feudal Window*'.

I am also indebted to the publishers New Age Books for their interest, patience and encouragement in bringing the chronicles into the public domain by publishing it under their banner. It serves to encapsulate history vividly at the microcosmic level of a fief.

My wife Amrita, herself a scholar of history, has always been thoroughly supportive of my tiresome efforts to bring the dream of publication to realization, believing that it had the blessings of all ancestors and would prove invaluable not only for future generations but also those curious to learn little known facts about the life and times of the colourful chieftains in our feudal past. My only regret is that my father is no longer with us to see his dream realized, though surely he would have the satisfaction of knowing that the chronicles of the clan includes him as the last ancestor.

# Preface

This is a tale of extraordinary survival of a clan over a millennium. The chronicles of the Mertia Jagmalots traces their origins to their progenitor Rao Duda of Merta and through him to the Rathore clan of Rajputs. The martial Rajputs, according to many historians, descended from the Scythians who ruled large tracts of northern India in the early centuries of the first millennium A.D.

While it is true that we are all in a sense survivors down from Adam, but to be able to trace a lineage over six hundred years on the basis of historical records puts such survivors in a remarkable category of their own. Tracing the history of one family in the sub-clan assumes historical significance as a study of a microcosm representative of numerous feudatory families across Rajasthan which have braved the vicissitudes of history to survive meaningfully to the present day. The story of one family then becomes the story of every such family with minor variations.

We see how they faced one challenge after another with the changing dynasties and empires in the region and at the central seat of power. We observe how they withstood the hegemonistic ambitions of the regional super powers and the overlordship of the Delhi Emperors expressed through their Governors at Ajmer. The manner in which they succeeded in fending off the bigger fish in their neighborhood, forever seeking to swallow them or learnt to deal tactfully with the whales from Delhi, emerging remarkably intact into the present times, constitutes the theme of our narrative. Where no trace remained of the great dynasties of the Khiljis, the Tughlaks, the Lodis and even the most glorious of them all, the Mughals, all being consigned to history, the fiefs and principalities of Rajputana amazingly survived improbable odds right into independent India. While most did so under the umbrella of the regional overlord, the Maharaja, those in the vicinity of Ajmer were more remarkable for having managed to do so without one, swimming so to speak in the protective shadow of the Mughal leviathan and later in the train of yet another that displaced it, the British. The Mertia Jagmalots, descendants of Jagmal hailing from Merta, are one such family and this book, in the latter half seeks to chronicle their extraordinary career.

In doing so we begin at the beginning, postulating the origins of the Rajputs, then tracing the history of its major clan the Rathores, the circumstances and the manner of their migration to Marwar ( Jodhpur), making it the seat of their power. From Marwar we move to Merta where a branch of the Rathore line under Rao

Jodha's brilliant son Duda carved out further territory. We then dwell on Duda's descendants focusing attention on his grandson Jagmal. We pursue the career of his descendants the Jagmalots till the conquest of the small principality of Masuda near Ajmer. The remainder of the book dwells on the life and times of the family which held that principality right up to Indian Independence.

Their chronicles have been presented in the backdrop of all events occurring in North India at the time, interweaving the career of the family with the changing historical scenarios within the region and beyond at the level of Imperial India. We thus see the unfolding of Indian history from the eleventh century to the present day in the context of the role of the Rajput protagonist and finally its one offshoot, the family to which I belong. It is quite an amazing story which would provide the general public an extraordinary perspective of history viewed as it were from the base upwards rather than a macrocosmic survey, the bird's eye view, which often fails to bring out the actual effect of events down at the individual level. Being replete with rare anecdotes the chronicles bring to life the sweep of historical events through a most engaging and vivid presentation, much like the unfolding of a story.

# Part I

## The Origins

# 1

# The Rajputs

The Sanskrit word Raj-Putra or its abbreviated form Rajput, in common usage, means royal sons, sons of kings, or sons of nobility. Rajput clans in India can be found in several regions, from Gujarat in the west to Rajasthan in the north-west, Madhya Pradesh in Central India, Utter Pradesh in the north and further east in Bihar and Orissa.

While the Rajputs generally hold that they are Aryan by descent, most historians are inclined to the view that they are descended from the Scythians who ruled North West and northern India for about four centuries till the rise of the Gupta Empire, in 395 A.D. The Indo-Scythians or 'Sakas' mentioned in the Puranas, were a Central Asian nomadic tribe inhabiting the banks of the river Javartes near Farghana. Their first forays into India took place with Alexander in 320 B.C. They founded their first kingdom at Gandhara, displacing the Indo-Greek dynasties. In 70 B.C. they set up their capital at Taxila. Later when the Kushan dynasty drove them south, they came to establish kingdoms in the Punjab, Sindh, Kashmir, parts of Uttar Pradesh, Saurashtra, Kathiawad, Rajasthan, Malwa and northern Konkan in Maharastra.

The Scythians were a warlike tribe of horseman whose branches spread to parts of Europe and Scandinavia on the one hand and Afghanistan and India on the other. Their creed was sun-worship with Zoroastrian influences. In India their beliefs were transformed by Brahmanical thought and practice and by the close of the fourth century A.D. they became totally indigenized, merging with the Hindu mainstream. Historians generally hold that they then metamorphosed into the Rajput and Jat clans in the areas where they had ruled. The horse and reverence for the Sun continued to play a significant role in Rajput and Kshatriya lore, with a campaign of conquest being preceded by the horse-sacrifice or Ashvamedh Yagya and the clans designating themselves as Solar races, the *Suryavanshis*. While the bulk of Rajputs is believed to have descended from the 'Saka' rulers, historians also maintain that some may have had Hun origins.

The Rajputs are one of the premier martial races of India and have been renowned in history for their exceptional chivalry, unmatched valour, gallantry, fearlessness, courage and martial skills combined with strict honour codes for conducting warfare and being gracious and magnanimous in their treatment of the vanquished.

The Rajput values honour above all else and is quick to take offence if by word or deed this core value is violated. To redress it he will duel, nurse vengeance for a lifetime, go to war or engage in subterfuge. To protect it, he will sacrifice life, limb, love, family, wealth and kingdom. Rajput women are equally committed to preserving honour and do not hesitate to encourage and impel their men to guard it with their lives and themselves are ready to sacrifice everything to defend it.

The Rajput is also known for his loyalty towards his family, clan, friend or master. His loyalty does not waver or diminish no matter what the circumstances or challenges confronting him. For instance the bond of brotherhood symbolized by the 'Rakhi' band tied ceremoniously by a sister on his wrist obliges him to give his life if needed to honour it by protecting her in adversity. As a loyal retainer none can compare with a Rajput whose service to the master is an article of faith and comes before self. While these virtues are commonly held in esteem in India, for the Rajput they are not mere ideals but core values to be accorded the highest priority before all other considerations of family, wealth or well being. Some people regard the Rajput as naïve, impractical and intemperate for not being more pragmatic and realistic in prioritizing his values. It is however this very naivety and uncompromising commitment in upholding values considered sacrosanct that defines the Rajput character.

There are several shrines dedicated to Rajputs who fell in battle as 'Jhunjhar' (pillar of sacrifice), the mythic phenomenon of a gallant soldier who continued to ride for a while in the heat of battle despite being decapitated. Indian history is replete with tales and legends of such extraordinary valour and incredible feats of martial prowess of Rajput clans, making them formidable and invincible adversaries. In north India they constituted the greatest challenge to foreign invaders and adventurers who hearing of the fabled riches of the lands south of the Himalayas, time and again sought to plunder, destroy, convert and rule India which came to be known as the 'Golden Bird'.

At every stage in Indian history it was the Rajput resistance which sought to stem the alien invasions from the north. It was the Tomar Rajputs at Delhi and Kanauj in 1018 A.D. who faced the first major Islamic invasion of Mahmud of Ghazni, a Turk with the missionary zeal of a new convert. The Gulf Arabs trading along the Saurashtra and Malabar coasts had already carried tales of the fabled riches of India. Mahmud combined religious passion with a desire to plunder. Between 1000 and 1026 A.D. he launched sixteen campaigns in India from the Indus to the Ganges. The Tomars joined forces with Anandpal the king of Punjab. Their armies were such as Mahmud had never encountered. But the army stampeded with an unfounded rumour of the flight of Anandpal's elephant and victory for the Indian Kings was suddenly and gratuitously converted into defeat with tragic consequences for India which was plundered and desecrated.

Two centuries later it was the Chauhan Rajputs led by the great Prithviraj who stood like a rock to face the invasion of the Afghan Chief Mohammed Ghori in 1175. Ghori at first faced serious reversals, almost losing his life and beat a hasty retreat back to Kabul. Unfortunately the victory was short-lived and on his second invasion an year later Ghori's shrewd maneuvers and strategies succeeded in routing the much larger army of Rajputs. Fortunately he also did not seek empire and leaving behind a viceroy at Delhi returned with his plunder to Kabul.

Once again the Rajputs recovered their losses and while Delhi saw a succession of Muslim dynasties come and go, the Sisodias of Mewar and Rathores of Marwar consolidated their conquests becoming the bulwark against foreign aggression.

The third Islamic invasion, that of Timur in 1398, yet another plundering raid, further weakened the Delhi Sultanate but had no impact on Rajputana whose chiefs were hardly aware that a major invasion had come and gone.

Baber's invasion in 1524, his conquest of Punjab and then Delhi was however of a completely different category. The Mughals had not come merely to plunder but to establish an Empire in Hindustan and they did not intend like their forerunners to return to their mountain homeland. At Khanua, the invader faced the greatest challenge yet in five centuries. Rajputs from every clan and kingdom in Rajputana joined as one to block the bid for empire. Despite a mammoth force of the best warriors of Hindustan, procrastination and prevarication lost the day and yet again the Rajput bulwark failed to thwart alien ambition to rule the subcontinent.

Maldeo of Marwar once again, fifteen years later, sought to stem the tide of Islamic rule by challenging the might of the upstart Afghan Chief Sher Shah who had displaced the Mughals but failed on account of growing dissensions within Rajput ranks. Finally it was only Mewar that sought to resist the unrelenting expansion of the Mughal Empire but the storming of Chittor under Uday and victory over his gallant son Pratap at Haldighati removed the last remnants of Rajput resistance in 1567.

With the growing power of the Mughal Empire, Rajput kingdoms and principalities finally acknowledged that a dependent status was preferable to being totally dispossessed of their fiefs and kingdoms. This pragmatic approach led to alignment with the Mughals and acceptance of their suzerainty. Close cultural economic and military ties followed, remodeling an erstwhile adversary into the very sinews of empire. The Mughals equally realized the value of allying with the Rajputs to maintain and expand their empire. The Mughal armies were often commanded by Rajputs. Rajput soldiers were employed in large numbers and on several occasions the Commander-in-Chief of the Mughal army was now a Rajput. The Mughal emperors came to trust Rajputs more than their own clansmen for providing their personal and imperial guard because they were exceptionally trustworthy, honorable and loyal and deceit and betrayal were not characteristic of their behaviour.

The Mughals were so impressed by the qualities and strengths of the Rajputs that they even sought marital alliances with them, despite the barrier of religion. In a few generations the Mughal emperors came to have more Rajput blood flowing in their veins then Central Asian, Persian, Turkish or Arab. Rajputs thus became the backbone of the Mughal Empire and even the bigoted emperor Aurangzeb had several Rajput generals in his command.

If Rajput men are renowned for their gallantry, chivalry and loyalty, Rajput women equally are famed for their virtuosity, chastity, piety and resolute strength of character. Their stoic support for their men in battle is legendary. There is the famous ballad 'Sainani' or souvenir sung romantically all over Rajasthan to show the stern mettle which a Rajput lady is made of. It relates a somewhat macabre tale of a Rajput chief just married who is loath to go to battle leaving behind his bride whom he adores. Time and again he leaves but is barely able to reach the doorway or castle gates or mount his horse but returns to have one more look at his beauteous bride. She scolds him to go and do his duty in battle. Finally he weakly agrees, but halfway to the battlefield he sends a messenger to his bride pleading for a souvenir. The messenger returns with the 'Sainani'. A silver salver covered with brocade cloth. He eagerly uncovers it to find the severed head of his bride - her stern message being that she is shamed by his adulation which distracts him from his duty in battle. Then getting the message loud and clear, with a heart of stone and iron resolve he does his bride's bidding and launches himself furiously and single mindedly into battle.

If the ballad of 'Sainani' shows the martial fervour of the Rajput lady, the story of Meera Bai no less shows the strength of her piety. Meera renounced the splendours of the palace, breaking every code of staunch orthodoxy which prohibited public appearance for royal ladies, to become a travelling mendicant singing songs of divine love for Lord Krishna, which are even today sung the length and breadth of the land, making her better known than her gallant male counterparts.

Then again when the husbands of Rajput women were vanquished and killed in battle, history is replete with legends of their committing 'Johar' by jumping en masse into flaming pyres and being martyred rather than submitting to the dishonour of being taken captive, converted and turned into concubines. Equally there was the heinous practice of Rajput women ending their lives on the funeral pyres of their deceased husbands as 'Sati' to prove their love and singular devotion, rather than accept a life of lonely widowhood. This heinous practice was frowned upon by the erstwhile colonial masters the British and eventually outlawed in independent India.

But let us not imagine that the Rajput lady was inflexible when challenged by the circumstances of a changing world. If she had the courage to join her deceased husband on a funeral pyre or to commit mass suicide, rather than become a slave of the conqueror, she displayed extraordinary courage in defying tradition by giving her consent to wed an emperor from an alien culture and religion when this suited the requirements of real politik. Raja Bharmal of Amber's daughter not only became the empress of India but eventually the mother of the emperor Jehangir. Her presence at the Mughal court produced a rare cross-cultural fertilization bringing the refinements of Mughal culture, architecture, arts, crafts, technology and style of governance to the Rajput court, while carrying in turn Rajput culture, traditions, customs, festivals, cuisine and sensibilities, reflecting the aspirations of the Hindu masses, to the Mughal court. The Rajput lady would bring with herself her entourage of hand maidens, cooks, tailors, bearers, priests and more important her kith and kin who would eventually find positions of influence and power in the empire. The brother of Akbar's Rajput queen, Man Singh rose to become the Commander-in-Chief of the Mughal armies and numerous Rajput youth joined the imperial service. The result was an intimate cultural fusion and what is sometimes overlooked a unique and far reaching fusion of blood lines. It also contrariwise became the practice for the daughters of Rajput Mughal princesses to wed the princes of Rajwara. The strong Mughal influences on Rajput fashion, dress and etiquette are evident from the changing style of miniature paintings, depicting Rajput princes in postures, headgear and dress which increasingly began to resemble those of the Mughal aristocracy.

The Amber princess was no exception. Marwar followed Amber in giving its princess royal in marriage to Akbar's heir apparent Jehangir, himself the son of the Amber princess. Jehangir improved upon Akbar's record and married two Rajput Princesses, one the daughter of Udai Singh Maharaja of Jodhpur and the second his mother's niece the daughter of Raja Bhagwan Das of Amber Their offspring were Shahjehan, the next emperor and his elder brother Khusrau respectively. We see that several Mughal Princes were the offspring of Rajput mothers. Even the bigoted emperor Aurangzeb's first wife according to one source was a Rajput princess.

These conjugal influences made their impression on Mughal thinking in the treatment of the Hindu populace. The abolition of the hated Jazia tax on Hindus by Akbar is a sterling example. The secular thinking of Akbar and his pantheistic curiosity to learn about Hinduism and other religions were doubtless engendered by the fact that his premier queen empress maintained a temple in the palace for personal worship and would anoint his forehead and sword with vermillion, the auspicious Hindu mark for sanctifying a new undertaking. Later followed the translations of the Mahabharat and Ramayan into Persian with abundant illustrations in the Razaknama to enable Akbar to familiarize himself with the epics. His son Jehangir was also well versed in Hindu thought and believed that the origins of Sufi thought appeared to lie in the Upanishads. Akbar's great grandson Dara Shikoh echoed his grandsires deep interest in Hindu scriptures when he sought not only to immerse himself in the study of Vedanta and the Upanishads but to undertake their translation into Persian.

In short, the role played by the courageous Rajput ladies in the sixteenth century Mughal court, despite the hostility of the Turkish, Arab, Persian and Central Asian coteries in the harem had profound reverberations, transforming the very tenor of Mughal rule over India. Their sacrifice in this respect was no less remarkable than their martyrdom in flames.

Thus on the one hand the Rajput emerges as the glorious Indian counterpart of the Greco-Roman Heroes of the classical age, the European Crusaders, the English Knights, the French Musketeers and Japanese Samurai of medieval history, while on the other, his female aspect shines out as the epitome of sacrifice, strength and piety, a veritable Joan of Arc.

The Rajput policy of strategic compromise, when faced by an indomitable foe, paid abundant dividends. Their kingdoms, principalities and fiefs survived superbly from one empire, that of the Mughals to the next, the British and right into independent India. The kingdoms and principalities were persuaded to accede to independent India and in return were treated by the new dispensation with generosity and grace. The Rajput Maharajas and Chieftains survived thus into the twentieth century making their contributions to independent India as their genius would allow. Independent India had a Rajput Prime Minister, several Governors, Chief Ministers, Ministers, Bureaucrats, Ambassadors, diplomats, a Commander-in-Chief, Generals, Admirals, Soldiers, Jurists and Judges, Academics, members of legislatures, Journalists, thinkers and writers, becoming a new bulwark for the nation, the strong sinews of the new state, given their prodigious and splendid heritage and history.

# 2

# Origins of the Rathore Clan

The Rathores are one of the premier clans of the Rajputs. They are mainly concentrated in the area of Marwar, Bikaner and Merta in Rajasthan with Jodhpur as their principal city. They are also settled in Gujarat, Madhya Pradesh and Uttar Pradesh where they held kingdoms, fiefdoms and Jagirs or otherwise were soldiers and retainers in the employ of their overlords. Their main occupation aside from their martial activities was farming.

According to several historians the Rathores are descendants of the Rashtrakuta dynasty which ruled parts of North and South India in the medieval period, in particular the Rashtrakutas of Manyakhet in Maharastra (which acquired its name from the Rashtrakutas) and the Rashtrakutas of Lat in Gujarat.

The Rathores on the other hand make mythological claims to descent from Lord Rama's son Kush. They also describe themselves as a solar race, the 'Suryavanshis'. According to James Tod a British administrator turned historian and genealogist of Rajput clans in the early nineteenth century, the first so called solar dynasty according to the Puranas was that of Manu, the Hindu equivalent of Adam, as the first created man. From his descendants came king Ikshvaku, the ancestor of Lord Rama, the divine Avatar and his twin sons Luv and Kush.

There is also the mythic tale of the first Rathore being created from the spine of Indra, the god of thunder and the administrator of the heavenly world of Indra-Lok. Furthermore, like all caste Hindus, they associate themselves with a pre-historic sage – in their case Gautam, as a member of his extended family over the ages. Thus at prayers when a Pandit demands to know which Gotra (extended family) they belong to, the Rathore's reply is, 'Gautam Gotra'. This is important in determining their identity and whom they can marry and with whom marriage is prohibited. It is generally held among most caste Hindus that marriage within the Gotra is tantamount to incest and totally prohibited. Traditionally a Rathore would therefore never marry another Rathore even if there is no direct familial connection for generations. Thus, the name of a Rathore's wife would never have been suffixed with 'Rathore'. Rather, in times past, the wife would still be referred to in accordance with her clan name: if she was a Shekhawat she would be called Shekhawatniji, if she was a Sisodia, as Sisodiniji and so on. In rural India even today young lovers who transgress this prohibition of marriage within the 'Gotra', at the least would find themselves ostracized by society and in rare cases even be hounded and killed by their relatives for having brought shame and ridicule to the family name.

We now return to the Rashtrakutas of Lat. Around 1080 A.D. this branch of Rashtrakutas established dominion over Kanauj on the banks of the Ganges. At the time it was called Gadhipur and they began calling themselves Gahadavals. The dynasty ruled Kanauj for a little over a hundred years, their last ruler being Jaichand who was killed during the invasion of Mohammad of Ghor in 1194 A.D.

An historical survey of northern India in the twelfth century A.D. reveals three prominent kingdoms, all Rajput, holding sway over vast territories. About 170 years had passed since the first major Islamic onslaught of the Afghan king Mahmud Ghazni, which began with destruction, plunder and wanton killing of 'infidels' in their hundreds of thousands and destruction of Hindu kingdoms and concluded with the sack of the great Shiva temple of Somnath in Gujarat, a great centre of Hindu pilgrimage. But Mahmud had no intention of making permanent conquests. His aim was merely the killing of 'infidels' and plunder of India's enormous treasures.

Hindu kingdoms however revived and established themselves in the succeeding century. Prithviraj Chauhan's dominion included Delhi and Ajmer and all the territory westward to the Indus and all lands from the foot of the Himalayas to the Aravalli hills. The Chauhans had succeeded the Tomar rulers at Delhi.

The other great kingdom was that of Kanauj under Jaichand, extending north to the foot of the Himalayas, east to Banares and across the Chambal river to Bundelkhund, coming into contact in the south with Mewar. The kingdom of Kanauj was at this time in its most glorious phase and its ruler Jaichand was in the process of celebrating his supremacy over lesser chiefs by demanding that they pay him homage at Kanauj. According to legend, Prithviraj refused to do so and this had enraged Jaichand who made a golden statue of Prithviraj as a doorman and installed it at the gates of his palace.

It is evident that the two great Hindu monarchs of Delhi and Kanauj were bitter adversaries, though the legend of abduction of Jaichand's daughter by Prithviraj at her 'Svayambara', the ceremony where she was to select a spouse from the gathered chiefs by garlanding him, is discounted by most historians as a romantic tale invented by Prithiviraj's renowned bard Chand Bardai in his famous ballad 'Prithviraj Raso'. The Raso goes on to condemn Jaichand for treacherously inviting the Afghan King Mohammad Ghori to invade India and subdue Prithviraj, which is equally discarded by historians as fictional, considering that Ghori didn't spare Jaichand either. However the Raso's praise for Jaichand's greatness as a monarch with the title of 'Mandalica', his subjugation of the kings of the North, 'West of the Indus', making eight tributary kings prisoner and that his dominion extended south to the river Narbada, appear more credible, particularly since it is praise for an arch enemy.

The third kingdom was that of Mewar. The House of Mewar is believed to have one of the longest surviving lineages among the Rajput clans. The eminent chronicler James Tod, a political agent of the British for Western Rajput states in the nineteenth Century, in his classic 'Annals and Antiquities of Rajasthan' that Mewar (along with Jaisalmer) was the only dynasty of Rajputs which outlived eight centuries of foreign domination "in the same lands where conquest had placed them", whereas the others in northwest Rajasthan were 'relics of ancient dynasties drawn from their seats of power". It is for this reason that the Ranas of Mewar are held in such high esteem. They claim descent from Lord Rama's other son Luv and are styled 'Hindva Surya', the glorious sun of the Hindus. They are believed to have resided at Lahore, earlier known as Luv Kot, emigrating later to Dwarka in Gujarat. When expelled from Saurashtra they came to be known as Gehlots and later after establishing the kingdom of Mewar in southern Rajputana, as Sisodias.

It is in such a setting that the second great Islamic invasion shook the foundations of India, ending the rule of independent Hindu kingdoms and installing at Delhi, the heart of the Empire, Islamic rule for over six centuries till it was replaced by the British Empire in the nineteenth century.

Mohammad Ghori burst into India in 1175, addressing himself first to subduing Arab colonies along the Indus and the remnants of the Ghaznavid chieftains. By 1182 he had overrun the whole of Sindh right up to the seacoast. Peshawar fell in 1179 and by 1184 he ravaged Lahore and Sialkot. He thus rid himself of all Muslim rivals in India first before turning to the Hindu kingdoms. He then faced the great monarch Prithviraj Chauhan who had succeeded the Tomars at Delhi and Ajmer. Prithviraj was supported by the might of Mewar whose prince Sanarsi was married to his sister. A mighty battle was fought in 1191 at Narain near Panipat just north of Karnal in which Ghori was vanquished and fled in panic back to Afghanistan. The Sultan could not forget this disaster and humiliation and confessed that he "never slumbered in ease nor waked but in sorrow and anxiety". Resolute in his determination to fight the 'infidels', he launched his second massive invasion with a formidable force of 120,000 Afghans, Turks and Persians and met Prithviraj again at Narain in 1192. This time through superior covert strategy he routed Prithviraj's army and pursued the fleeing Prithviraj, capturing and killing him - in his words, finally 'sending him to hell'. The prince of Chittor his ally and brother-in-law, Sanarsi, was also killed in battle.

Here James Tod an ardent sympathizer of the Rajputs says:

"Rajasthan exhibits the sole example in the history of mankind, of a people withstanding every outrage barbarity can inflict, or human nature sustain, from a foe whose religion commands annihilation, and bent to the earth yet rising buoyant from the pressure and making calamity a whetstone of courage. How did the Britons at once sink under the Romans and in vain strive to save their groves, their Druids or the altars of Bal from destruction. To the Saxons they alike succumbed, them again to the Danes; and this heterogeneous breed to the Normans. Empire was lost and gained by a simple battle and the laws and religion of the conquered merged to those of the conquerors. Contrast with these the Rajpoots; not an iota of their religion or customs have they lost though missing a foot of land.... Mewar alone, the sacred bulwark of religion, never compromised her honour for her safety and still survives her ancient limits and since the brave Sanarsi gave up his life, the blood of her princes has flowed in copious streams for the maintenance of this honour, religion and independence. What nation on earth would have maintained the semblance of civilization, the spirit or the customs of their forefathers, during so many centuries of overwhelming depression, but one of such singular character as the Rajpoot?"

It is evident that Tod held Prithviraj and Sanarsi in high regard as the heroes who sought to withstand the foreign onslaught, but blames Jaichand for treachery and national infidelity in not joining their forces, indeed collaborating with the invader which ultimately led deservedly to his own destruction. Here he obviously relies on the Chauhan bard's 'Raso' version of events which we have seen are not authenticated by most historians in regard to Jaichand's treachery. Suffice it to say that the rivalry and deep antagonism of the great Hindu kings at this crucial phase in Indian history was probably the reason why Ghori on his second invasion succeeded in routing them one after another paving the way for Islamic rule in India.

Following the victory at Narian, Ajmer, Hansi and Sirsuti were annexed amid general slaughter and looting and Qutubuddin Aibak, a slave was appointed Viceroy of India at Delhi. Mohammad Ghori returned from Ghazni a year later and now faced Jaichand in 1193, inflicting a crushing defeat on him on the Jamuna. Jaichand drowned in the river while escaping. Thus did the ancestor of the Rathores lose his kingdom and his life but his descendants were destined to carve out a kingdom, far west in Marwar, no less glorious than their forefather's at Kanauj. How this came to pace we shall presently see.

# 3

# The Conquest of Marwar

After the death of Jaichand his son Harishchandra ruled the area immediately around Kanauj. The kingdom was now greatly reduced in size. Meanwhile the slave kings at Delhi sought to consolidate their hold. After the death of Ghori his slave Qutubuddin Aibak had declared himself king. Qutubuddin continued the Muslim expansion and soon nearly all of Hindustan north of the Vindhyas was under Muslim sway. To commemorate his victories he built the famous Qutub Minar, victory tower, which to this day stands magnificently tall as a reminder of this first major Muslim ingress and establishment of rule in India. Aibak survived his master only a few years, killed by a fall from his horse playing polo in 1210.

His slave Altamish, deposed Aibak's incompetent son and assumed kingship. Like Mohammad Ghori and Qutubuddin he too was of Turkish extraction. The Turks being the latest converts to Islam had the unbounded zeal of the convert. Altamish set out to further consolidate Aibak's conquests and in the process attacked Harishchandra. The remaining territory of Kanauj proper also then slipped from his control.

Thus eighteen years after Jaichand's death two of his descendants, probably grandson and great grandson began their migration from the land of their birth in 1212. According to Tod the two, Saitram and Seoji with two hundred retainers journeyed west to seek their fortunes afresh in the western desert knows as Maru Sthal or 'dead lands'. They intended first to make pilgrimage at Dwarka on the west coast. En route at Pushkar, another major centre of pilgrimage near Ajmer, Seoji sought to redress the grievances of Brahmins suffering harassment of Muslim chieftains. Moving further north, the royal emigrants were received by the Solanki chief at Kaloomund just west of Bikaner. He showered them with kindness and hospitality. The expectation was that the Rathore force would help him in combating his enemy the Jareja chiefs of Phaolra. With Seoji's help the Jareja menace was overcome but Saitram was killed in the campaign with a sizable number of Seoji's retainers. The Solanki chief in gratitude proposed a marital alliance and gave his sister in marriage to Seoji with an impressive dowry. Seoji then proceeded to the great pilgrimage centre of Dwarka. On the way he encountered the remnant Jareja forces and totally routed them.

As he grew in confidence and wealth his ambitions also rose. He began by attacking the chiefs entrenched along the dry desert river Looni, desirous of acquiring land at any cost. First the Dabhai chief was assassinated at a feast. Then the Gohil chief was eliminated by the sword. Finally Seoji planted the Rathore standard along the Looni and acquired a land base. Later he was invited by the Brahmins of Pali, a prosperous commercial centre forty miles southeast of present day Jodhpur, to defend them from tribes of Mers and Meenas who frequently raided the town. Seoji overcame the menace and gained the confidence and loyalty of the influential citizens of Pali. Eventually the city was brought under his overlordship. With these acquisitions Seoji succeeded in establishing a land base for the Rathores and obtaining their first foothold in Marwar. He was killed fighting Muslim chieftains in 1273 A.D.

For some 250 years after Seoji's death his clansmen and descendants engaged in frequent warfare to expand their base in Marwar with fluctuating fortunes till Rao Jodha took Mandor in 1453. Fortunately they had bountiful progeny and single minded ardour to settle and expand their territories. In the process they sought to displace the local clans of Gohils, Parihars, Pawars, Bhatis, Sodhas, Sankhalas, Solankis as also the tribal Meenas in addition to defending their gains from covetous Muslim chiefs of neighbouring Malwa and Gujarat. Mandor was taken more than once and lost and regained. Other areas acquired and lost were Sojat, Nagaur, Jalor, Sambhar, Merta, Phalodi and even Ajmer. What is evident is that the Rathore clans were determined to expand and hold at whatever cost their hard won gains in Marwar.

Rao Chunda was the next great stalwart to plant the Rathore banner at Mandor in 1382, slaying the Parihar rulers. Mandor was then the capital city of Marwar. From Mandor he assaulted the imperial garrison at Nagore successfully. Proceeding further south he occupied Nadole, capital of Godwar province. He accepted the offer of marriage to a Parihar princess. Chunda also gave his daughter in marriage to the Rana of Mewar. The great Rana Kumbha was her grandson.

Chunda's son had fallen out with the Bhati rulers in the north over the hand of a Mohil princess desired by both parties. The Bhatis were now bent on taking revenge against the Rathores. The Bhatis and their allies the Sankhalas aided by Salim the Governor of Multan invaded Nagaur. The Rawal of Jaisalmer conspiring with the Bhatis, offered his daughter in marriage to Chunda supposedly to end all disputes and restore tranquility to their lands. The marriage procession in fact was an army disguised in bridal finery. Chunda even as he realized that he had been duped was assassinated in 1424.

Chunda's legacy was that Rathore rule in Marwar had been established on a firm footing. In addition he had also contracted a strategic marital alliance with the august house of Mewar thus setting the stage for further enhancing the prestige and power of his clansmen.

The next notable descendant was Chunda's first born, Rinmal. He was of gigantic stature and a renowned athlete, clearly the most able of Chunda's sons, but not the favourite. He was persuaded to waive his rights to succession in favour of a younger brother Kanha. Disgruntled, he left Marwar early to seek his fortunes elsewhere and approached Rana Lakha of Mewar. The growing might of the Rathores of Marwar had become a cause of concern for the Mewar rulers. In the dispossessed Rinmal, the Rana saw an opportunity to sow the seeds of dissension within Rathore ranks. Heretofore the Rathores had acted as one and in the process had succeeded in enlarging their dominions.

Rana Lakha welcomed Rinmal and showered him with favours including the Jagir of Dunlo for his maintenance. It was at Dunlo that Jodha the shining star of the Rathores, was born in 1428 and grew to maturity. Rinmal became a loyal retainer of the Mewar Rana and did not disappoint him in furthering the fortunes of Mewar. Soon he led the Rana's forces and brought Ajmer under Mewar's authority. As relations grew warmer, Rinmal with his father's approval offered the hand of his sister for Rana Lakha's eldest son and potential heir Rawal Chunda. The proposal was made in Lakha's court with the traditional offering of a coconut. Rawal Chunda was then away on tour. The Rana in jest remarked in open court while stroking his moustache that he presumed that the offer was not for him adding 'I do not suppose you send such a plaything for an old grey beard like me'. The court burst into laughter with the joke circulating among the nobility.

On his return Rawal Chunda heard of the incident and was not amused. Being deeply offended by his father's jest he refused the marriage proposal. Incensed by his son's unreasonable and obstinate refusal to accept the match and seeking to avoid grave insult to Rinmal and Marwar he chastised Chunda for being over sensitive over trivia and said he would marry the princess instead on condition that Chunda renounce his succession to the throne in favour of any son born to the princess. Chunda's injured sensibilities were further aggravated by these demands and in a fit of Rajput bravado he swore by the family deity Eklingji to honour his father's wishes. Thus an inadvertent and facetious remark changed the very course of Mewar's history displacing a competent and worthy heir with one who had not even been born.

This episode throws into bold relief the volatile temperament and mercurial character of the Rajput. Rajput history is replete with events where a chance remark, trivial jest or act of omission aroused a wholly disproportionate reaction leading to banishment of progeny, fratricide, patricide, refusal to marry at the ceremony itself, lifelong vengeance or declaration of war. Trivial incidents so affected the Rajput heart and mind as to supersede every other sensible cause, interest, ambition and objective in favour of irrationally dedicating life, limb and destiny to the narrow purpose of redressing an imagined insult or dishonour.

Hansabai princess of Marwar married Rana Lakha, the 'greybeard' while Rawal Chunda his eldest son nursed ill founded grievances of his own making. Lakha and Hansabai were indeed blessed with a son, Mokul. Before proceeding to fight a righteous war to have the holy city of Gaya vacated from Muslim occupation, Lakha installed the minor Mokul as his heir. Lakha was killed in the campaign to free Gaya.

Thus we see Rawal Chunda forsaking his succession to Mewar, the right of his progeny to the kingdom and subverting Mewar's history over an assumed slight, despite his father's protestations. Rana Lakha's son Mokul from the Rathore princess was likewise killed by his uncles for merely asking 'Uncle what tree is this' which they interpreted as an allusion to their mother's descent from a clan of carpenters. Later we see Mokul's son Rana Kumbha banishing his eldest son for 'impertinent curiosity' in wanting to know why lately he had began to wave his sword in circles over his head before sitting on his throne. One cannot even imagine what circumstances may have transpired at the Mandor court which denied the able Rinmal his succession in favour of a younger brother, leading to his migration to Mewar with serious consequences for both Marwar and Mewar.

Rawal Chunda assumed the regency under the guidance of the Queen Mother. As a token of his sacrifice in forsaking his rightful succession to the throne it was agreed that the symbol of the lance of his fiefdom Salumbar would henceforth be affixed on the seal of Mewar and it remains there to this day. However, the simmering suspicious and acrimony of the Queen Mother eventually drove him in frustration to relinquish the regency and migrate in a huff to the court of Mandu in Malwa where he was received with honour and given a distinguished appointment.

Upon his departure the Queen Mother's kinsmen hastened to fill the vacuum. First Rinmal's son and her nephew Jodha assumed charge of important posts. Rinmal followed along with numerous other clansmen in taking up positions of authority. Rinmal now at the helm of affairs sought to avenge the murder of his father by having Salim, Governor of Multan assassinated and the Bhatis faced a punitive campaign. Rinmal also conquered important regions of Marwar including Nadole, Jaitram and Sojat annexing them to Mewar. In 1627 he unseated his brother Satta from the throne of Mandor bringing it under Mewar rule. Thus he avenged the denial of his rightful succession to the throne of Marwar. He also assisted the young Rana Mokul in invading Nagaur, Jalore and Sambhar in Marwar and fought a battle with Mohammed the son of the Sultan of Gujarat. In 1433 as we noted earlier, Mokul's uncles assassinated him and as his son Kumbha was only six years old, Rinmal continued to govern Mewar as Regent. As the Sultan of Mandu had given refuge to one of Mokul's assassins he marched against him and inflicted a crushing defeat on him in 1437. He also successfully led the Mewar armies against Sarangpur in Malwa, Nagaur, Gagaraun and Narara in Jaipur and Ajmer.

As his influence rose in Mewar, courtiers complained to the Queen Mother that he appeared to have intensions of usurping the throne. What lent credence to these rumours was his insensitive behaviour at court. He is said to have so grown in self-esteem that on several occasions he casually sat on the throne of Mewar with his grandson on his knee. Meanwhile to add to Hansabai's suspicions regarding her brother's intensions, a brother of Rawal Chunda who had sullenly isolated himself in his fiefdom, was assassinated. Rinmal sent him a poisoned dress of honour in an apparent bid at reconciliation which he was obliged to don. The Queen Mother convinced that her own kin were now quite untrustworthy and intoxicated with power, in a reversal, sought Rawal Chunda's help. Chunda readily schemed to return in disguise with a force at a festival at Chittor. He stormed the citadel having gained entry by subterfuge and slew every Rathore he could lay eyes upon. The unsuspecting Rinmal was murdered with the connivance of the woman in his arms, as attendant of the Queen Mother.

Jodha however escaped the pogrom and arrived in Marwar with only seven retainers. Rawal Chunda's hatred and vengeance was not yet assuaged and he pursued Jodha. Chunda took Mandor by surprise and occupied the capital of Marwar in 'sweet revenge'. Jodha, prevented from returning to Mandor, sought the support of a renowned Rajput warrior, both ascetic and soldier, with a considerable following in the region. Another anchorite Pabooji on his coal black steed, who is today revered as a deity in Rajasthan was also approached for support. Soon he found himself strong enough with the support of these heterogeneous elements to attempt a recovery of his capital. Rawal Chunda's son was taken by surprise and killed. Another was also pursued and killed near the border with Mewar. With the recapture of Mandor in 1453 he then proceeded to wrest Sojat from Mewar in 1455. Gaining in confidence and strength he then sought to avenge his father's assassination and attacked Chittor and plundered Mewar. The Rana of Mewar Kumbha then launched a counter invasion of Marwar but apprehensive of an invasion by the Sultan of Malwa, negotiated a treaty with Jodha fixing the boundary of Mewar and Marwar. With this demarcation, which continued to hold virtually to the present day, Rao Jodha had consolidated his kingdom. He performed his coronation ceremony in 1458 at Mandor.

In the following year 1459 he laid the foundation of a new fortress and a new city at its base which he named Jodhpur, the city of Jodh after his own name. It was in fact an ascetic Jogi living in a cave nearby who directed Jodha to create his castle on Jodagir, the 'hill of strife', hitherto known as Bakurchuria or 'the birds nest'. This was a cliff top projection some four miles south of Mandor, the ancient traditional capital of Maru-desh or Marwar. It was also strategically a good choice, being virtually inaccessible and providing its master both with a unique security and a commanding view of the entire countryside from its desert fastnesses right up to the Aravalli range. Thus was Jodhpur founded with the blessings of a Jogi, with a strategic and impregnable location, visible from afar as the flagship of the Rathores. The chiefs of numerous clans and tribes that had ruled Marwar heretofore were no longer in evidence. The Parihars, Sankhalas, Chauhans, Gohils, Dhabais, Sindhals and Jats were more or less consigned to history and the few remaining did so as the retainers of the Rathores.

James Tod speaks of the ever growing numbers of the Royal family: "Such was the abundant progeny of the princes that the limits of their conquests soon became too contracted". In three generations we see first Rao Chunda with fourteen sons, Rinmal with twenty four and Jodha no less, with fourteen. The choicest parts of the emerging Marwar had already been apportioned amongst them and Tod adds "it became necessary to conquer fresh fields in which to sow the Rathore seed". And that is precisely what ensued through the extraordinary efforts and genius of his sons. Of Jodha's many sons, the most eminent were Duda and Bika who were responsible for greatly expanding Jodha's territorial domination over Marwar. In 1462 at his command, Duda proceeded to annex the important region of Merta adjacent to Ajmer with 360 villages from Mallu Khan the representative of Sultan Mahmoud of Mandu (Malwa).

In 1465 another son Bika conquered the area in the north called Jangalu, infested by marauding tribal brigands. Later it came to be called after his name as Bikaner.

In 1467 Jodha annexed Nagor. A year later the great Rana of Mewar, Kumbha was treacherously killed by none other than his son Udai. Afraid of the disaffection of his nobles and fearing a rebellion, Udai sought to appease his powerful neighbour by seeking his neutrality in return for ceding Ajmer and Sambhar with its rich resources of salt from the Salt Lakes.

Jodha outlived the foundation of his new capital thirty years. When he died in 1489, his kingdom embraced Mandor, Phalodi, Pokharan, Mahema, Bhadrajun, Sojat, Godwad, Jaitaran, Sambhar, Ajmer and a large part of Nagaur. Merta, Bikaner and Chhaaper - Dronpur were in the possession of his sons Duda, Bika and Bida. Thus the boundaries extended from the Aravalli hills in the south to Hisar in the North and in the west touched the state of Jaisalmer. Writing in 1832 Tod adds "in less than three centuries after their migration from Kanauj, the Rathores, issues of Seoji spread over a surface of four degrees of longitude and the same extent of latitude, or nearly eighty thousand mile square and they amount at this day, inspite of the havoc occasioned by perpetual wars and famine to 500,000 souls".

We now shift our focus from the House of Jodha to that of his son Duda with whose descendants we shall mainly be concerned in sketching the history of a Rathore sub-clan which has acquired the definition of Mertia Jagmalots or descendants of Duda's son Jagmal, hailing from the region of Merta.

Here a brief recapitulation of events would be in order to see what was transpiring in the imperial neighbourhood while the Rathores had been consolidating their rule in Marwar. Following Mahmoud Ghazni's invasion in 1192, the imperial capital had seen a succession of Muslim dynasties succeeding one another. The slave kings had been followed by thirty years of rule by the Afghan Khilji dynasty and ninety year rule by the Tughlaks. Timur Lang's invasion in 1398-99 had once again shaken and wrecked the power of the central authority beyond repair, shrinking its authority to the area immediately surrounding the capital city of Delhi. The Sayyid's who filled the vacuum for about thirty years dissipated their energy by fighting among themselves with resulting anarchy. Some stability however returned with the emergence of the Afghan Lodi dynasty. Bahlol Lodi who supplanted the last feeble Sayyid in 1451 showed both energy and wisdom in eventually restoring the imperial fiat as far as Bihar and his able successor Sikander extended it right up to Bengal.

But at the time of Duda's emergence, Behlol Lodi had only managed to bring back some semblance of governance to the area around Delhi. The rest of India now had numerous independent states both Hindu and Muslim. Between Delhi and Bengal there was the kingdom Jaunpur under Muslim rule. Two more powerful kingdoms had established themselves, breaking away from the central authority under local Sultans in Malwa and Gujarat. In Malwa Dilawar Khan, a descendant of Ghori had extended his territory over most of the old kingdoms of Malwa and shifted the seat of authority from the ancient capital Ujjain to Mandu along the slopes of the Vindhayas. Mewar continued to play a significant role as a buffer against the ambitions of the Muslim chiefs of Malwa and Gujarat, with Marwar now growing in strength and stature further north. The rulers of Malwa and Gujarat constantly sought to expand their territory into Rajasthan and in the process had to deal with Mewar's first line of defence.

In 1435 Rana Kumbha was the shining star of Mewar, renowned for his valour and ability to defend Mewar. Mahmud Khilji, Vazir of Malwa after murdering the grandson of Dilawar became Sultan and revived the kingdom of Malwa to its greatest strength. He then proceeded to seize Ranthambore and Ajmer in 1435. The Sultans of Malwa and Gujarat then formed a league against Kumbha and invaded Mewar in 1440 with a powerful army. Rana Kumbha however delivered a crushing defeat on them and celebrated his victory with the construction of a memorial tower at Chittor, the 'pillar of victory' which proudly stands resplendent to this day. The measure of his victory can be judged from the fact that he carried the Sultan of Malwa, Mahmud Khilji back to Chittor as a prisoner. The Sultan was kept as prisoner for six months before being magnanimously and unconditionally set free. Akbar's chronicler Abul Fazal speaks of Kumbha's greatness and magnanimity in releasing a captive foe. Tod comments on the Rajput character which the incident highlighted: "Such is the character of the Hindu: a mixture of arrogance, political blindness, pride and generosity. To spare a prostrate foe is the creed of the Hindu cavalier and he carries all such maxims to excess". But judging from the fact that the Malwa Sultan joined Kumbha and helped him defeat the imperial forces at Jhunjunu shortly thereafter indicates that the magnanimity shown was not without strategic purpose and later paid ample dividends.

It was in such a setting, with the imperial power in Delhi in decline after Timur's invasion and the star of Mewar at its zenith, that Duda in 1462 captured Merta from the Sultan of Malwa's viceroy Mallu Khan.

# Part II

## The Mertias

# 1

# Branching Out

## Rao Duda (1462 – 1515)

On the death of Rao Jodha in 1489 his sons Duda, Bika and Bida declared themselves independent of Marwar and assumed the title of Rao. Rao Sital succeeded to the throne of Jodhpur.

In 1490 Merta was faced with a great famine. In order to provide relief to the poor cultivators, Duda asked the rich merchants of Sambhar to make donations. Their arrogant refusal forced him to take punitive action and confiscate their assets. The Seths appealed to Mallu Khan to come to their assistance. He readily marched from Ajmer to attack Duda, hoping thereby to regain Merta. Duda asked Rao Sital to assist him in confronting Mallu Khan. Mallu Khan's soldiers while encamping at Kosana attacked 140 women Tijania pilgrims celebrating Gangaur. Incensed at this sacrilege Rao Sital and Duda attacked Mallu Khan, rescuing the Tijanias but Sital was killed in action. On his death his brother Shuja succeeded to the throne of Marwar. This was challenged by Bika who was an elder brother. The threat from Mallu Khan to Merta had however been averted.

In 1493 there was yet another occasion for Duda to confront Mallu Khan when he deceitfully imprisoned Duda's brother Varsinh at Taragarh fort after inviting him for a friendly conciliatory meeting at Ajmer. The Rathore forces once again stood together against a common enemy. Duda, Bika and Shuja's forces joined together and marched on Ajmer to punish Mallu Khan and free their kin. Varsinh was released and Mallu Khan sued for peace which was accepted on condition of future good behaviour. Varsinh however subsequently died on account of slow poisons administered during his captivity.

Always concerned to maintain close links with the prestigious House of Mewar, Duda arranged the marriage of his eldest son Viramdev with the daughter of Rana Raimal, the exiled heir of Rana Kumbha. It was Raimal who finally succeeded in dethroning his brother Udai who had so treacherously killed the great Kumbha and occupied the throne of Mewar. Viramdev's son was later given the fief of Ghanerao in Godwar by the Rana. Among a handful of Mertia principalities surviving into the twentieth century, Ghanerao can lay proud claim to being one.

Friendly cooperation between the Rathores of Jodhpur and Merta continued and in 1498 Rao Duda assisted Shuja in ousting the Sindhals from the Jetaran region which became part of the kingdom of Jodhpur. In 1510 the Sultan of Malwa encouraged by his viceroy at Ajmer, marched into Rajasthan and came right up to Sambhar. The combined forces of Jodhpur, Bikaner and Merta stood as one in staunch defence, forcing the Sultan to retreat.

Early in the sixteenth century we see a generational change taking place with the death of Bika in 1500, and both Duda and Shuja in 1515. In 1509 Rana Sanga succeeded to the throne of Mewar, whereas Rao Ganga succeed in Marwar and Viramdev son of Rao Duda at Merta.

# 2

# Legendary Princess of Merta

## Meera Bai (1498 - 1547)

The Annals of Merta history would remain incomplete without due homage to its extraordinary princess Meera. This flower that bloomed on its genealogical tree has ennobled it no less than the chivalry and heroism of its sons in winning battles and kingdoms and being martyred in pursuit of glory. Her mystical quest left its indelible mark on the very soul of India, being venerated universally and for posterity as a poet saint without equal.

Duda's fourth son Ratan Singh was the honourable father of the legendary Meera Bai. Thus all descendants of Duda, Mertia clansmen, can claim kinship with this extraordinary spiritual phenomenon of the sixteen century, renowned the length and breadth of India. For them she is as much a revered ancestor as any of those in the male genealogical table and therefore we feel obliged to give her pride of place in this Merta narrative.

Given the marital alliances in preceding generations with Mewar, in particular that of Viramdev, son of Duda and her uncle, with Rana Sanga's aunt and even earlier Rao Rinmal's sister's marriage to Rana Lakha which produced in two generations the stalwart Rana Kumbha, Viramdev inherited the best of relations with Merta's powerful neighbour Mewar.

Viramdev succeeding Duda as Rao of Merta took the initiative to marry his niece Meera to Rana Sanga's eldest son Bhojraj to further cement their bonds. Tod according to several historians has erroneously claimed that Meera was married to Rana Kumbha, which would be almost a century before her estimated birth. Several notable historians have placed Meera's birth in 1498 when her father was about eighteen years of age. Meera would therefore have been about eighteen when she married Bhoj Raj in 1516. Her husband died within seven years of the marriage in a battle. She lost her father soon thereafter when he joined Rana Sanga in the great battle of Khanua against Baber in 1527.

Memorial Statue of Meera Bai at Nagaur

Here let us pause to consider how the princess of Merta and wife of the Mewar Rana's eldest son became a mendicant and later found a place among the galaxy of poet – saints of the period. The sixteenth century saw an important development in the evolution of Hinduism. The stoic and esoteric practices of an earlier age had consisted on the one hand in elaborate Vedic rituals for empowerment and invoking divine grace and on the other, meditation and Yoga for spiritual and physical evolution with philosophical debates and introspections on the nature of divinity as in the Vedas and Upanishads. The sixteenth century saw the emergence of devotional prayer as an additional attribute of spirituality. Rather than the intellect and ritual, this movement called 'Bhakti', sought mystical communion with the divine through expression of love – the heart came into play rather than the mind. Devotion through love was considered now to be superior and a more direct form of worship. Thus, suddenly a number of poet – saints emerged all over India, voicing and espousing the new spiritual language of love. Tulsi Das, the devotee of Rama, Sur Das, that of Krishna, Kabir Das of a more abstract spirit and Guru Nanak, embracing all elements of devotion, filled the minds and hearts of devotees with their songs and verse.

Even as a child Meera's intense spiritual inclinations were clearly evident. Several legends have grown about her extraordinary life, first in childhood in Merta later as wife of the Rana's son in Mewar and still later as a wandering mendicant singing songs of mystical love from place to place across North India. One legend speaks of her asking her mother about her relationship to the idol of Krishna she worshipped. She believed her mother when she in jest exclaimed that Krishna was her groom. Her poetic creations are full of the intense spiritual love she felt for the Lord, as one who was waiting eternally for her lover, looking over the rooftops of the castle to see if his caravan was on its way to her.

In another song she tells her mother of a dream in which she weds her beloved Krishna. She sings of "waiting in the Monsoon rains, with heart fluttering, hearing the Lord's (Hari) wet footsteps approach". In yet another song she claims to have bought Lord Krishna after carefully weighing his worth and that some people said she had paid too little, others that she had paid too much.

At Merta it is evident that she was encouraged in her spiritual pursuits by her doting grandfather Rao Duda in whose loving care she grew up as the strange and saintly little princess. Duda himself was a great devotee of Lord Krishna and would have contributed to her spiritual development rather than hindered it. Later, even as a bride at the Mewar royal court her mystical obsession received indulgent acceptance by her father-in-law the great Rana Sanga who was not unfamiliar with his grandfather Kumbha's deep devotion to Lord Krishna. Such deep spirituality was not uncommon among both men and women of the age as the Bhakti movement took the land by emotional storm.

Even her husband Bhojraj is not portrayed as an intolerant tyrant who would be offended by her attitude, rather legend has it that he was indulgently amused and permissive of her obsession. When he asked her who her husband was, she is said to have remarked that she belonged only to the lord of the soul (Prannath). In a song she replies "Mine is only Giridhar Gopal, there is no other". Bhojraj did not survive long enough to test her inflexible commitment to a journey of the spirit.

However, after his death and that of Rana Sanga in 1527, when she also lost her father, the atmosphere in the Mewar court changed dramatically. Sanga was succeeded by his second son Ratan, a fairly temperate and accomplished individual in 1530, but he was killed in a quarrel over a maiden. He was succeeded by Vikramaditiya in 1535.

Vikramaditya was of a completely different metal. He had a turbulent nature, insolent, passionate and vindictive, fond of watching wrestling matches of prizefighters on whom he lavished gifts, failing to give any respect even to his nobles. He considered his brother's window to be a nuisance, weird, eccentric and bizarre. When he learnt of her total disregard for conventional norms of the Royal Zenana (Ravala), the ladies wing, in straying out of the palace to pray and sing at temples in town, keeping the company of ascetics in violation of the code of royal female privacy, it was no longer an issue of eccentricity only but serious breach of court etiquette and family honour. Rumours abounded and the situation was now scandalous. He forbade her from leaving the palace, which she defied. He even forbade her from worshipping Lord Krishna whom he believed was the source of her obsessive behaviour. This too she defied. He finally sought to rid himself of the nuisance by poisoning her. According to legend she drank the cup of poison with a smile and miraculously remained unaffected. Several of her songs allude mockingly and disparagingly to the Rana's atrocities. In one she defiantly asserts: "Ranaji, I shall continue to sing songs of praise of Lord Krishna, if the king turns away from me, the town will keep me but if the Lord turns away where would I go then". Again in another song she says "Ranaji sent the cup of poison, Meera drank it with a smile". Yet again "Ranaji I find dishonour sweet, I shall continue to walk strangely". Though never named, it is clear that the Rana referred to was the intolerant Vikramaditya.

However to be fair to Vikramaditya, notwithstanding his intemperance, one cannot but admit that in the sixteenth century it must have appeared scandalous and outrageous for a lady of the royal house, a widow, to venture out singing and dancing with ankle bells in the streets and temples in the company of men-folk albeit ascetic or saintly, when even as late as the fifties of the twentieth century they were required to observe strict 'Purda' on outings. Then, lace curtains were drawn within their motorcars and if they ventured out on foot, could only do so within the confines of canvas tent barriers to shield them from public gaze. Whatever the rationale, her lyrics and songs of protest against the Rana's atrocities have damned him for all eternity. One has to be careful, not to be at cross purposes with a saint.

Thus far, her uncle Viramdev had remained committed to the strong links with Mewar, always accompanying Rana Sanga on his campaigns. After Sanga's death the ill-treatment of Meera made him disenchanted and he ultimately called Meera away from Chittor to Merta. She continued on her spiritual quest becoming more and more involved and committed. In 1538 upon Rao Maldeo's (ruler of Marwar) capture of Merta from Viramdev she is said to have become a wandering mendicant with a large following, moving from place to place singing songs of divine love. According to legend she met the poet-saint Tulsidas, author of the famous Ramcharitmanas. Another popular legend speaks of the emperor Akbar, hearing of her poetic and musical genius, becoming desirous of seeing her in person. His great court musician Tansen accompanied him incognito and joined the congregation to hear her sing. Later when they came to seek leave, she recognized Tansen and rebuked him for singing for the emperor rather than the Lord of the soul.

Meera's wanderings took her to Vrindavan, the holy centre of Krishna worship. Later she moved to Gujarat composing many poems in Gujarati. Meanwhile, after the assassination of the intolerant Rana Vikramaditya, Udai the youngest son of Rana Sanga and Meera's youngest brother-in-law eventually succeeded to the throne. Udai felt remorse for the mistreatment of Meera and hearing of her presence at Dwarka sent a delegation of Brahmins in 1547 to invite her to return to Chittor. The Brahmins waited while she entered a Krishna temple for prayer. According to legend all that was found of her at the temple was her string instrument the 'Ek Tara' and her apparel, for she had finally gained her wish of union with the Lord and merged with him leaving no trace behind. No trace indeed is also found of her either in the annals of Mewar, her name being expunged from them. Neither is there a painting or even a sketch defining this great personage to be found anywhere. It is only on the basis of legend about her uncommon beauty and saintliness that latter day artists have sought to portray her with a saffron robe covering her head with a 'tanpura' string instrument in her hand.

However her lyrics and poems did not suffer the same fate of oblivion, being passed on from one faithful generation of worshippers to another, from Gujarat, Rajasthan, Mathura and Vrindavan to Bengal in the east where a cult following is still evident today. Her poems are not only in the native Rajasthani dialect, but as she moved on her meanderings, appear in Brij, the language of Mathura, the heart of Krishna worship, to Gujarati and Bengali. For centuries since, every worthy singer has used her lyrics and music to give sanctity to their art. In the present day one finds that from the most popular singers like the Mangeshker sisters Lata, Usha and Asha, to others like Vani Jairam, Chaya Ganguli, Kavita Krishnamurti, Devaki Pandit, Anuradha Paudwal, Hema Desai, Sadhana Sargam and classical singers like Kaushiki Chakrabarti, Shubha Gurtu, Ashwini Bhide, M.S. Subalakshmi, Shubha Mudgal and numerous others have all paid homage, singing Bhajans, Thumris and complete Raga compositions with her lyrics in praise of Lord Krishna.

M.S. Subalakshmi was the first in the fifties to both star as Meera in a feature film, as also sing her songs, followed by Hemamalini in the eighties in Gulzar's film Meera in colour.

Today that homage is also paid in Mewar where at Lord Krishna's Srinathji temple her memory is celebrated, even if belatedly. For a time however the House of Mewar pledged not to bring a bride from the Mertia clan. That extraordinary Rathore princess of Merta however today is better known beyond Rajasthan, than any of her male Rajput counterparts, as her name has become an indelible part of popular memory of the poet-saints of the Bhakti movement.

# 3

# The Dawn of Empire

## Viramdev (1515 - 1544)

Viramdev succeeded Duda at Merta in 1515 at the age of thirty eight. For Viramdev a close alliance with Mewar remained an article of faith throughout his life. Marital ties had created a strong bond between the two kingdoms. Viramdev's wife was a Mewar princess and his niece Meera had married the prince of Mewar. He therefore joined the Rana in all his campaigns.

The rivalry between Mewar and the Muslim rulers of Malwa remained a perennial issue. It will be recalled how Kumbha in 1440 had inflicted a crushing defeat on Mahmud Khilji of Malwa, taking him as prisoner and erecting a victory tower at Chittor to commemorate the event, though later in a fit of magnanimity he had released the Sultan. Since then Mewar's influence in Malwa had become supreme. A feudal chief of Malwa, Medini Rao of Gagnore exercised that authority as a representation of Mewar. When Mehmud II Sultan of Mandu was deposed by his nobles in favour of his brother Salih Khan, Medini Rao had intervened to restore him to the throne. But intrigues at the court set Mehmud against his benefactor, leading to the attack on Gagnore and the slaying of Medini Rao's representative. Rana Sanga then marched against Malwa to restore Medini Rao's authority. Viramdeo was invited to join the campaign which he readily did. The campaign was successful. The defeated Sultan sued for peace and surrendered his bejeweled crown in lieu of a peace treaty.

On another campaign, Sanga proceeded to help the ousted ruler of Idar, Raja Raimal against the Sultan of Gujarat. Other Rajput forces from Dungarpur, Jodhpur and Merta joined in support of the Maharana's campaign. The Raja of Idar was restored to the throne and the usurper Hakim Hasan of Idar fled but was pursued and killed. The Sultan of Gujarat then approached the Sultan of Malwa to combine forces with him to avenge the intervention of the Mewar Rana. Malik Ayaz commanding the force marched to meet the Rana's forces. Viramdev was again with the Rana in fending off the attack. Malik Ayaz lost courage, retreated and sued for peace. Rana Sanga fought no less than eighteen battles with the Sultans of Delhi, Malwa and Gujarat and in most campaigns Viramdev remained loyally by his side extending Merta's support.

Momentous developments were now on the horizon. The Mughals from Central Asia had consolidated their position in Kabul. Their young chief Baber now descended into Hindustan through the northern passes, much as had Ghori, Ghazni and Timur, but unlike them destined to create an incomparable empire in India. In 1526 Baber decisively defeated Ibrahim the last of the Lodhis at Panipat, killing him in battle despite the latter's formidable army of a hundred thousand men and a thousand elephants. Baber won against odds through sheer strategy, superior technology and the advantage of artillery, introduced in India for the first time. He then moved towards Agra, occupied the fort and took possession of the Lodhi treasures. At Delhi he had the Khatwa read proclaiming him as Emperor of Hindustan. He also built pleasure gardens and set up fruit orchards to 'civilize' the land. He was not allowed to indulge such botanical interests for long.

A more formidable foe than Ibrahim Lodhi now challenged his imperial ambitions. The might of Mewar, the last bastion of Hindu resistance which had managed over centuries to remain unaffected by the shifting fortunes of Imperial Delhi, was now reinforced by Sanga's unshakable resolve to take advantage of the decline of the Delhi Sultanate and become master of Hindustan. The formidable Rajput forces now advancing on Agra included Rao Ganga of Jodhpur, Rao Viramdev of Merta, Raja Prithviraj of Amber, Raja of Idar in Gujarat, the Rawal of Dungarpur, Kumar Kalyanmal of Bikaner, Raimal Rathore in command of the Jodhpur forces, the Rawat of Deolia and many other stalwarts. Hasan Khan Mewati and Mahmood Lodhi son of the vanquished Ibrahim Lodhi also made common cause and augmented the Rajput ranks. Baber estimated that the force now arraigned against him was no less than an army of two hundred thousand. He was also aware that this was no motley group of mercenaries but the finest 'pagan' warriors of Hindustan. The legendary might and heroism of Rana Sanga combined with the forces of all Hindu princess of Rajputana, their differences set aside for once, appeared as an insuperable monolith.

On Baber's own admission his followers were so demoralized by the adversary that "not a single person uttered a manly word, nor an individual delivered a courageous opinion". Even his court astrologer predicted defeat. On the fifth of 'Kartik' 1528 the Rana laid siege to Bayana and advanced to Khanua. The Mughal advance guard of fifteen hundred was decimated to a man and reinforcements met the same fate. In despair Baber sought to uplift the spirits of his army by destroying all wine flasks and vowing on the holy book not to touch wine again, declaring that he would conquer or perish.

When victory was clearly in sight for the Rajputs, it appears that fate clouded the Rana's judgement. Uncharacteristically and inexplicably the hero of numerous battles sought to negotiate rather than fight, allowing time for Baber's forces to regroup and win much needed respite. In the negotiations, Sanga offered that Baber could keep Delhi if Bayana became the boundary with Mewar and an annual tribute was paid. Matters procrastinated and there was no agreement. Baber finally attacked with a much smaller force. His artillery located in the trenches became a formidable factor in his favour. Superior strategy held the day. The Rajput losses mounted in a vain attempt to cross the entrenched artillery barrier. One by one Rajput stalwarts fell. The Rawal of Dungarpur, Ratan of Salumbar, Raimal Rathore, son of the Jodhpur chief, Ratan Singh Mertia father of Meera Bai, several Jhala, Parmar and Chauhan chiefs, Hussain Khan of Mewat and Ibrahim Lodhi's son Mehmood were all slain. It became an unprecedented rout. Rana Sanga himself was forced to retreat with most of his chiefs killed. He vowed gallantly never to return to Chittor till he was victorious. Baber did not ravage Mewar as it was the height of summer and with shortage of water he didn't wish to push his luck.

That year Sanga died a fugitive. It is suspected that he was poisoned by his retainers who felt that his bravado would prove their ruin. The heroic Sanga by the end of his valiant career would have been a fearful sight, having lost an eye in a quarrel with his brother, an arm in battle with the Lodhi Sultan, another limb mutilated by a cannon ball. He had as many as eighty wounds from action in battles in different parts of his body.

The battle of Khanua signaled the end of any ambitions which the Hindu or Rajput may have had of gaining empire or even independence and set the seal for ushering in the Mughals as empire builders in India. This was also the last occasion when Rajput unity stood cemented as a monolith against a common cause, which itself was a feat difficult to countenance. After the shock of defeat and the death of innumerable notable personalities there was no possibility of such solidarity ever arising again to effectively counter an invader.

Henceforth Rajput chiefs sought to promote their individual narrow agendas. Rathore chiefs never again joined forces to face the common menace of the Sultans of Gujarat or Malwa. With the central power at Delhi growing stronger by the day and planning to expand the empire, the chiefs of Rajputana could no longer ignore the developments in their neighbourhood. The Mughals confronted the Rajput Kingdoms and brought them under their suzerainty one by one, occasionally facing some inconsequential resistance. Eventually they were forced to become instruments for maintaining the empire. The Rajputs now confronted their tormentors the Sultans of Malwa and Gujarat not at their own instance but at the behest of the Mughals. As the Mughal Empire rose in eminence the Rajputs became its staunch supporters and even joined their bloodlines with the Mughals in the ultimate gesture of solidarity with what had been an adversary.

What the rout at Khanua immediately spawned was Marwar's ambitions following the succession of Rao Maldeo in 1532. Maldeo characteristically began his career by pushing his mild mannered father Rao Ganga from his seat on a balcony causing his death.

What had made Rao Ganga intolerable for his son was his pacifist approach towards the vassal lords of Marwar and his counsel that all issues with Rathore brethren should be settled with peace and amity. Maldeo wanted to bring all the vassal fiefs under his unquestioned authority. He also wished to annex the Rathore kingdoms of Bikaner and Merta. After dealing with the vassals he attacked Bikaner and Jait Singh the ruler was killed. Bikaner for a brief period came under Maldeo's rule. Next he set his sites on Merta. Viramdev's simmering feud with Maldeo had originated in a battle jointly fought where a prize elephant, a trophy of victory became a bone of contention. Viramdev refused to hand over the elephant to Maldeo. Maldeo now sought deceitfully to divert Viramdev's attention elsewhere by inviting him to assist him in ousting the refractory Sindhals of Bhadrajune. While Viramdev proceeded on the expedition Maldeo surreptitiously attacked and overran Merta. Viramdev's cousin the Thakur of Rian, put up a strong resistance recovering Merta and hastened to inform Viramdev of the treachery. A thoroughly dismayed Viramdev hastened back and recouped his position at Merta. From then on the animosity between Viramdev and Maldeo rose to new heights with serious consequences for both.

Meanwhile Bahadur Shah of Gujarat invaded Chittor in a successful campaign against the weak and vacillating Rana Vikramadidya, the tormentor of Meera Bai. The Queen Mother saved the day by offering a trophy earlier won by Rana Kumbha, the bejeweled crown of Malwa, in return for peace. Flushed with success Bahadur Shah now sought to undo Mewar's conquest of Ajmer earlier in 1505 by sending a force led by Shamsher-ul-Malik in 1535 to wrest Ajmer from Mewar. Viramdev in a counter attack seized Ajmer.

In 1538, Maldeo with a great force occupied Merta destroying and ransacking the town and fort. Then he turned to avenge the action of the Rian Thakur earlier in recovering Merta for Viramdev. Rian also fell before Maldeo and the Jagir was given to his vassal Bar Singh. Viramdev then attacked Rian and killed Bar Singh. This enraged Maldeo who then attacked Ajmer and captured it, sending his senior generals Jaita and Kumpa to pursue Viramdev. Viramdev fled with the generals in hot pursuit. Moving from place to place he ultimately sought shelter at the imperial fort at Ranthambore. In desperation he sought help from his former enemies the Sultans of Mandu and Gujarat but they declined any help.

The year 1540 saw momentous developments taking place at the heart of the empire. Baber's son Humayun had squandered his opportunities in procrastination, opium, wine and the harem, allowing Sher Khan an upstart Afghan courtier risen from the ranks to capture Bihar & Bengal and then to challenge the Mughal might. The battle at Chausa a year earlier was a harbinger of events to come and at Kanauj Sher Khan now assuming the title of Sher Shah routed Humayun, who fled first to Lahore and then sought asylum with the untrustworthy Maldeo. Rumours that Maldeo planned to surrender him to Sher Shah in exchange for the province of Gujarat decided Humayun in making an escape from Jodhpur eventually to Persia, losing empire to Sher Shah.

Maldeo had greatly extended his domain taking advantage of the conflict between the Mughals and Sher Shah. His frontier was now barely fifty miles from Delhi. Aside from the fact that he had temporarily given asylum to Humayun, Sher Shah viewed him as a primary threat to his imperial ambitions. He referred to Maldeo as "that accursed infidel".

Rao Viramdev of Merta and Rao Kalyan of Bikaner, both dispossessed by Maldeo of their kingdoms now made common cause with Sher Shah and sought his help to regain their principalities. Sher Shah was well inclined towards them for their support in helping him in the conquest of Gujarat, Mandu in Malwa and Ranthambore in Rajasthan. They advised him to invade Marwar and unseat the ambitious Maldeo.

Sher Shah was only too ready to do so. He marched towards Ajmer in 1543 en route to Jodhpur at the head of the largest army he had ever amassed and camped at Mangaliawas. A calculating and pragmatic strategist he was loath to rush into a battle. His precautions had paid him well in routing the Mughals themselves and he was not going to hurry in taking on the infamous Rajput warriors for gaining desert lands. For a month the armies stayed put, looking upon each other without action. Sher Shah began to feel desperation and considered retreating rather than risk his empire in a war with Maldeo, for what he termed 'a handful of barley' the only major produce of the desert lands of Marwar.

It was Viramdev, nursing strong grievances, who conceived a brilliant stratagem of deceit arranging forged letters to be planted in Maldeo's camp suggesting treachery from within the Maldeo forces. The letters as intended came into the hands of Maldeo, who as expected grew alarmed that he would be betrayed in a battle with Sher Shah. He summarily retreated to the safety of Marwar with the bulk of his army when he could easily have faced Sher Shah with fair chances of victory. Maldeo realized too late that he had been duped and repented his hasty withdrawal. But it was too late as he had lost the strategic advantage. Sher Shah then marched on Jodhpur and captured it in 1544, appointing a Kiladar, returning to Ajmer via Merta. At Merta Viramdev was reinstalled and Rao Kalyanmal likewise at Bikaner. Sher Shah's brief reign terminated at Kalinjar during a siege against the Rajputs when he was killed in an explosion. Later Maldeo reasserted himself capturing parts of Pali and Jodhpur in 1546. Eventually he recovered Phalodi, Ajmer, Pokhran and even Merta.

Viramdev died in 1544 shortly after being reinstalled at Merta. He had sixteen sons. Prominent among them were Jaimal and Jagmal, founders of dynasties in fiefdoms in Mewar and Ajmer. Their careers we shall dwell upon at length considering that the remainder of the book chronicles the history of a Mertia sub-clan, the descendents of Jagmal. A third son, Pratap Singh the issue of a Mewar princess became the progenitor of further Mertia dynasties. He was gifted the principality of Chanod by the Rana of Mewar.

One of his grandsons Anup succeeded at Chanod while two others Kishandas and Abhay acquired the fiefdoms of Ghanerao and Kotharia in Mewar. Their descendants today are well established in public life as politicians, farmers, executives and hoteliers of heritage properties. Scions of the Mertia clan dispossessed of their Merta heritage thus migrated making their fortunes elsewhere.

# 4

# The Hero of Merta

## Jaimal

Viramdev's eldest son Jaimal succeeded him in 1544 at the age of thirty six. Jodhpur remained under the occupation of the Delhi Sultanate for about a year and a half after Sher Shah Suri's victory over Maldeo. In 1545 however, after Sher Shah was killed at Kalinjar and his son Salim Shah succeeded, Maldeo drove the Pathans out of Jodhpur following the battle at Sojat. In 1546 he raided Merta, but with the support of Kalyanmal of Bikaner, Jaimal effectively repulsed the attack. According to Jaimal's chronicles, the Jaimal Vansh Prakash, Jaimal fought Rao Maldeo on twenty two different occasions.

After the battle of Khanua in which the Rajputs had united against Baber, Rajput differences resurfaced. Mewar and Marwar resumed their rivalry with Jaimal backing Mewar with the additional support of Kalyanmal of Bikaner. This was only to be expected considering that Maldeo had sought earlier to annex both Merta and Bikaner. It was only through the intervention of Sher Shah that both kingdoms had been restored to their rulers. It appears that Merta itself did not present a united front. There appear to have been rivalries between the two brothers Jaimal and Jagmal, as we find that the latter was often to be seen in the opposing camp.

After Sher Shah's death, the Afghans also fell into internecine conflicts with resulting fragmentation. Humayun now seized the opportunity to recover the empire. In 1555 he overran Punjab and then took Delhi and Agra. But before he could do more, a year later he died from a fall in his palace. His son Akbar who ushered in the Golden Age of the Mughals, had been born at Umarkot, a Rajput principality of Sindh where Humayun in flight from Sher Shah had sought refuge.

Haji Khan an Afghan of the Sur dynasty was still in control of the Mewat region around Alwar when Akbar succeeded to the throne. Akbar lost no time in despatching a force to displace this remnant of the Sur dynasty. Haji Khan, then retreated to Ajmer but made the mistake of looting some villages of Marwar.

Maldeo marched towards Ajmer to punish him. Haji Khan turned for help to Maldeo's rival the Rana of Mewar. The Rana led a big force of cavalry assisted by his allies Rao Surjan of Bundi and Rao Jaimal of Merta. The Marwar forces under Prithviraj of Bagdi were defeated. The Rana then demanded compensation from Haji Khan for the expedition which included payment in gold and the surrender of the renowned dancing girl Rang Rai. Haji Khan refused to oblige and in a quick turn around now sought Maldeo's help. Maldeo complied, sending a force which included Jagmal. There ensued a battle in 1557 in which the Rana was wounded and his army took flight. Pursuing his enmity towards Jaimal, Maldeo sent a big force to attack Merta, which was captured. He then attacked Badnore, a principality which the Rana had conferred on Jaimal with a thousand villages. This too was overrun. With the loss of Merta and Badnore, Jaimal turned to Akbar's chief courtier Shaifuddin, the Amir-ul-Mulk for help. In 1561 Jaimal marched with the Mughal army and laid siege on Malkot, a new city built by Maldeo after the destruction of the fort at Merta. Malkot was captured and Jaimal was reinstalled at Merta. Jaimal's patron Shaifuddin however revolted against Akbar, seized Ajmer and began fortifying it. A punitive force was sent to deal with him. Shaifuddin fled and his revolt was crushed. As Jaimal was a protégé of Shaifuddin, he too fell from grace. Jagmal his brother, who was now in Akbar's service, was rewarded by being installed as ruler of Merta in 1563 through an imperial fireman. Maldeo meanwhile had passed away a year earlier in 1562.

Jaimal remained firmly committed to the House of Mewar, more so after the loss of Merta, and his fiefdom of Badnore. Mewar was now more or less in splendid isolation in its mountain fastnesses, confident that the cliff top fort of Chittor was eternally impregnable and beyond the reach of the Mughals. Akbar meanwhile had assiduously wooed the Rajputs with extraordinary tact and consideration. First Amber and then Marwar had succumbed to power and sweet entreaty. Amber had even entered into a marital alliance with the Mughals. Marwar would follow suit. Most of the Rajput chiefs were now Akbar's vassals, their innate strength augmenting the might of the Mughal Empire as pillars would an edifice.

Udai Singh had ascended the throne of Mewar in 1522. Akbar vowed to bring to heel this last great pocket of Rajput resistance. In 1568 marching on Chittor with a large army he laid siege, building tunnels to approach the cliff fort at close range. While the Rana affected his escape, his brave feudatory chiefs vowed to defend the seat of honour with their lives. Among them were the Chauhan chiefs of Bedla and Kotharia, the Parmars of Bijoli, the Jhalas of Sadri, the Sisodias of Salumbar, the Rathore chief of Jhalore and the Tomars of Gwalior. But as Tod says in his Annuals "the names which shine brightest .... and immortalized by Akbar's own pen" were the pride of the Mertias, Jaimal of Badnore and Patta of Kailwa. Both were among the sixteen Umraos having highest positions in the Mewar court. Jaimal and Patta henceforth became 'household names'. Jaimal, boldly directing operations from the ramparts of the fort was killed by a shot from Akbar who recognized the great warrior. Akbar later boasted that his favourite gun 'Sangram' had not let him down.

The dying Jaimal, knowing all was lost, signaled the women folk to commit Johar and masses of Rajput ladies leapt into the flames as they had done earlier when Bahadur Shah of Gujarat had stormed the fort. In a gesture to their heroism or as a mark of victory over Mewar, Akbar had statues of elephants with the two heroes astride placed outside his fort at Delhi. The French traveller Bernier, visiting India in 1663, looking at the statues remarked "for this gallantry it is that even their enemies thought them worthy to have statues erected to them".

Thus died Jaimal, the pride of the Mertias, considered by Tod as "the bravest of the brave clans of Marwar". In his martyrdom Jaimal displayed unique chivalry, an indomitable spirit, unbounded courage and everlasting yearning for independence, going down in history as among the bravest of Rajput warriors.

Rao Jagmal

# 5

# Mughal Governorate at Ajmer

## Jagmal

It is evident that the careers of the two Mertia brothers Jaimal and Jagmal who succeeded Viramdev one after the other to the throne of Merta, were divergent. Jaimal after losing the confidence of the Mughals had committed himself to the cause of Mewar and because martyred as a hero at the hands of Akbar. The other, Jagmal an adherent of the statecraft of survival won Akbar's favour and ultimately succeeded to his father's throne. Mutual rivalries doubtless played their part in the choices they made. Whatever the outcome, the descendants of both branches of the House of Merta survived into the twentieth century, Jaimal's as the Thakurs of Badnore in Mewar and Jagmal's as the Raos of the Parganah of Masuda in Ajmer Merwara. Both branches are today well established in Independent India as academics, politicians, diplomats, executives and hoteliers.

Jagmal had thirteen sons and for the record, considering that this book is essentially a history of his descendants, it is necessary to name them, if for no other reason than for the benefit of their descendants. The eldest was Bhupati alias Hanumant Singh as he is referred to in the British Gazeteers in a mistaken translation of the Persian records. The others were Lad Singh, Bagh Singh, Kalla, Roop, Chattar, Tej, Paidas, Siha, Suja, Narayandas, Ashkaran and Jait.

At the time that Jagmal was recognized as ruler of Merta through imperial proclamation in 1563, the young emperor Akbar's dominion mainly comprised Delhi and the Punjab. He then launched his career of conquests over one territory after another. Ajmer had already been occupied by 1556. Gwalior fell in 1558. The Afghans were driven out of Jaunpur by 1561. His overbearing mentor Bahram Khan had been despatched into exile. The Rajputs had yet to be fully subdued, Gujarat and Bengal were still beyond his authority and Kabul was virtually independent. Orissa, Kashmir, Sindh, Kabul and parts of the Deccan had yet to become a part of a greater empire.

The young and strident emperor was impatient and while rewarding those who were responsible for successful campaigns he did not allow them to rest a moment on their laurels. Vassals were perpetually commanded to join hectic campaigns for expanding the empire. In the process many suffered wounds and lost their lives in the service of the empire.

In 1556 Akabar conquered Ajmer which was strategically located at the heart Rajputana. An able and energetic administrator, Hussain Kuli Khan in whom Akbar reposed great confidence was appointed as Subedar, Governor of Ajmer. The provincial capital Ajmer had now become an important Suba of the empire which the emperor would be frequently visiting to worship at the shrine of his patron Saint, Khwaja Muin-ud-din Chisti.

The medieval period was one of poor means of communication. The horse was the fastest. Other means of transport were the camel, the oxcart and the lumbering elephant. In the absence of any modern means of communication, not even a horse drawn carriage, the emperors did not frequent their domain except when necessary. The prerequisites were rebellion which needed an imperial presence in person, vacations to idyllic spots like Kashmir or pilgrimage for worship. Frequency of visits to Ajmer was for the last reason. The emperor in fact walked barefooted to the shrine from Agra on more than one occasion to express humility before the saint. There was an air of informality during his visits to Ajmer in contrast to the pomp, splendour, formality and court etiquette of the Delhi Durbar. Jagmal's sons and other Rathore scions would soon be conquering and settling fiefdoms in the vicinity of Ajmer acquiring influence far exceeding their prestige, size or revenues for the reason that their proximity to the Suba headquarters would assure them an opportunity to meet directly with the emperor, whereas even Rajas and Maharajas in normal course would have to struggle hard to obtain an audience after making long and tiresome journeys to the capital Delhi. Furthermore, the Ajmer Chiefs would not be constrained by an overlord Maharaja whose permission would have to be sought before seeking an imperial audience. All these circumstances would create fortuitous opportunities for more intimate interaction between mere chieftains and the emperor himself.

The Suba of Ajmer eventually came to incorporate all of Rajputana as the Rajput rulers one by one accepted Mughal Suzerainty. While the Rajas and Maharajas ruled in their respective domains at the pleasure of the emperor, Ajmer became the headquarters of the Mughal Suba for Rajputana. Initially however, the nucleus of the Suba comprised the city of Ajmer and the fiefdoms in its vicinity. To the west was Marwar, in the east Amber, to the south Mewar, north was Merta and further north Bikaner and Jaisalmer.

The Governor had perforce to rely on the chiefs of the neighbouring fiefs for daily administrative needs and resources, particularly during the frequent visits of the emperor. Naturally, close interaction and intimate contacts would develop providing direct access with the emperor's representative in the region. Ajmer remained the centre of the Suba during Mughal rule initially for about a hundred years. Later Marwar for a brief period occupied Ajmer but it reverted to the Mughals who made the ruler of Marwar Governor. Thereafter it kept changing hands between the Rajputs and the Marathas. Finally the Marathas ceded it to the British. It later became the seat of the British Resident for Rajputana. The continuing special status afforded the chiefs of Ajmer region an exclusive advantage in their dealings first with the Mughal Emperor and later through the Resident with the British Governor General and Viceroy. There was no intercession of an overlord ever in their interactions with the Mughal Subedar or the British Resident.

Hussain Kuli Khan the Subedar was aware that stability in the region and its development were more urgent than would have been the case in other Subas which the emperor was not likely to visit often. Law and order therefore became a matter of high priority. The matter of immediate concern was the lawlessness, plundering and looting by the Parmar Rajputs in an area some sixty miles south of Ajmer city in the Parganah of Masuda. Of late the depredations of the Parmar brigands had exceeded all limits when they attacked a Mughal Thana. The Parmars had gained ascendancy in the area with the connivance of neighbouring Mewar and felt free to ravage the region. This intolerable state of affairs could not be allowed to continue. The Governor's choice for punitive action to restore order in the region fell upon Jagmal, recently installed as Rao at Merta for his admirable services to the empire. He could be trusted and Merta was also conveniently in the immediate neigbourhood of the Parganah of Masuda. The Padishah's orders were for ending the menace for good. The Mewar connection of the freebooter was added reason for taking precipitate action against the protégés of a recalcitrant adversary.

Jagmal had once again to prove his mettle and loyalty to the Padishah. It was around 1563 soon after his investiture at Merta that he therefore ordered his son Bhupati to lead the campaign to evict the Parmars from the Parganah. With this campaign begins the chronicles of his descendants, the Mertia Jagmalots.

# Part III

## Chronicles of The Mertia Jagmalots

# MERTIA JAGMALOT GENEOLOGICAL TREE

*KANAUJ*

JAICHAND (1173 – 1194)

HARISHCHANDRA (1194 – 1225)

*MARWAR*

SEOJI (1212 – 1273)

(After several generations) CHUNDA (1395 – 1424)

RINMAL (1427 – 1438)

JODHA (birth1428 – accession 1453 - death 1489)

*MERTA*

DUDA (1462 – 1515)

VIRAMDEV (1515 – 1544) | RATAN

JAIMAL | JAGMAL (accession 1563) | MEERA BAI (1498 – 1547)

*MASUDA*

(The Mertia Jagmalots)

BHUPATI (1563 – 1583)

NARSINHDAS (1583 – 1623)

JHUNJHAR SINGH (1623 – 1650)

AJAB SINGH (1650 – 1684)

MAUN SINGH (1684 – 1700)

SULTAN SINGH (1700 – 1713)

JAI SINGH (1713 – 1761)

RATAN SINGH (1761 – 1784)

BHAIRON SINGH (1784 – 1806)

DEVI SINGH (1806 – 1843)

SHEONATH SINGH (1843 – 1863)

BAHADUR SINGH (1863 – 1904)

BIJAI SINGH (1905 – 1938)

NARAYAN SINGH (1938 – 1992)

# 1

# Macrocosm to Microcosm

We now move from the macrocosmic survey of the history of the Rathores to the microcosm of the chronicles of its sub-clan the Mertia Jagmalots who settled in the principality called Masuda in the vicinity of Ajmer. The Mertia Jagmalots are so called because they are the descendents of Rao Jagmal hailing from the region called Merta.

The study would throw into relief the career and fortunes of a single Rajput family in the backdrop of six centuries of its ancestry which we have already traversed. This study of the lineage and destiny of a single dynastic entity over a thousand years, it will be acknowledged, would comprise quite a unique and engaging biographical exercise.

The case study would have value in providing a representative sample of the identical historical patterns of innumerable similar fiefdoms across Rajasthan. It would show the manner in which territories were conquered and settled, mode of acquisition of legitimacy from an overlord or through imperial investiture, nature of services required to be rendered to the suzerain power, fragmentation of the estate and spawning of smaller fiefs, adoption from anterior branches of the family tree on failure to produce a male issue, nursing of ambitions by all branches however remote that failure of the main line would provide them an opportunity to succeed to the throne, struggles for succession resulting in conflicts within the family, court intrigues and assassinations, defence against external threats, adjustment with changing circumstances resulting from arrival of new overloads, survival from one imperial dispensation to another, the emergence of such dynasties finally into an independent India which shed the feudal order in which they had been reared and striving ultimately to making their contribution in a democratic republic with the weight of an extraordinary lineage and heritage behind them. It would be the case study of a genealogical marvel, highlighting the art of survival across a millennium.

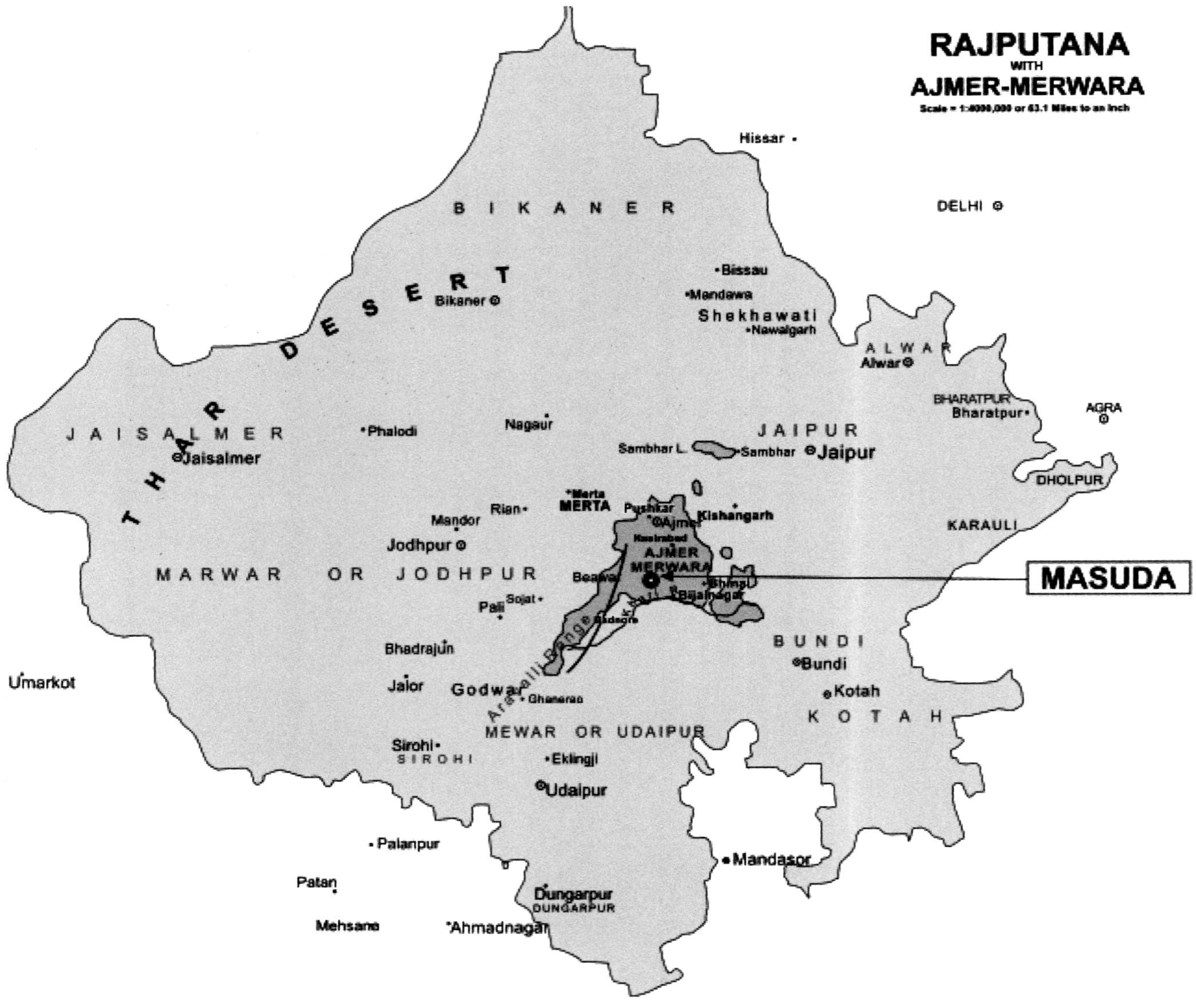
RAJPUTANA
WITH
AJMER-MERWARA
Hissar
DELHI
BIKANER
THAR DESERT
Bikaner
Bissau
Mandawa
Shekhawati
Nawalgarh
ALWAR
Alwar
BHARATPUR
Bharatpur
AGRA
JAISALMER
Jaisalmer
Phalodi
Nagaur
JAIPUR
Sambhar L.
Sambhar
Jaipur
DHOLPUR
Merta
MERTA
Pushkar
Ajmer
Kishangarh
KARAULI
Mandor
Rian
Jodhpur
AJMER
MERWARA
MASUDA
MARWAR OR JODHPUR
Beawar
Sojat
Pali
Bijainagar
Aravalli Range
BUNDI
Bundi
Bhadrajun
Kotah
Umarkot
Jalor
Godwar
Ghanerao
KOTAH
MEWAR OR UDAIPUR
Sirohi
SIROHI
Eklingji
Udaipur
Palanpur
Mandasor
Patan
Dungarpur
DUNGARPUR
Mehsana
Ahmadnagar

# 2

# The Conquest of Masuda

## Bhupati Singh (1563 - 1583)

It was around 1563, soon after Jagmal's investiture at Merta that in pursuance of the Subedar of Ajmer's concerns, be ordered his son Bhupati to lead the campaign to evict the unruly Parmars from the Parganah of Masuda. Bhupati proceeded on the campaign with seven hundred horse and an additional Mughal force provided by the Suba headquarters at Ajmer. He was accompanied by his brothers Lad Singh, Bagh Singh and Kalloji. A pitched battle took place for eight hours in which the Parmars were vanquished at Nimbahera village which was raised to the ground except for a Shiv temple which stands to this day marking the spot. Bhupati's descendents to the present day make offerings in homage at the temple. The British Gazetteer contains a record of the successful campaign by him in ousting the Parmars from the area for good.

As hardly anything remained standing as Nimbahera, wishing to establish a base, Bhupati planned to build a fort to secure his position. However, the first priority after having accomplished the assignment was to seek audience with the Emperor and receive due recognition. Bhupati was unable to get the Governor to facilitate this as Hussain Kuli Khan after Maldeo's death was busy trying to subdue Marwar. Maldeo's chosen successor Chandrasen refused to acknowledge Mughal suzerainty and the Subedar after capturing the Jodhpur fort was now in hot pursuit of the fleeing Chandrasen.

In the Subedar's absence the task of patrolling and maintaining order at Ajmer had fallen upon Rao Jagmal and Bhupati. He then asked his brother Bagh Singh to go to Amber and request Raja Bharmal to assist in securing an audience with the Emperor. While nothing came of this, Bagh Singh thereafter remained in Amber state having suitably impressed the Raja and became a retainer of the House of Amber. Rulers were always on the look out for talented and brave warriors to strengthen their court. Thus we find today that Jaipur State has several non-Kachwaha Rajput Chiefs in important principalities like Kanota, Gijgarh and Naila. Bagh Singh was later given the Jagir of Buda-Dewal.

Bhupati's other brother Lad Singh settled in an area neighbouring Masuda. He named the estate Baghsuri having witnessed a fight between a tiger and a wild boar at the spot where he built his castle. Lad Singh's descendents have distinguished themselves in several fields. The last chief, Onkar Singh held important positions during the British Raj and after independence his son Ajay Vikram Singh retired as Secretary of Defence in the Government of India.

After victory at Nimbahera, Bhupati proceeded to quell the depredations of the Bhil tribes who harassed caravans along the trade route from Gujarat to Malwa. He built a Thana at Bhinai which is called Bhupat-Sal. This campaign was undertaken by him in 1563-64 before the arrival of Chandrasen, the displaced son of Maldeo from Marwar. Chandrasen eventually ousted the Bhil Chief Mandalia and conquered Bhinai. His descendants became the premier chiefs in Ajmer in terms of status and protocol while Masuda remained the wealthiest estate of the region. Chandrasen's exploits and defiance of the Mughals have led several historians to compare him to Maharana Pratap for independence of spirit and the courage of his convictions though the annals of Marwar scarcely mentions him in deference to the sensitivities of the branch which succeeded to the Marwar Gaddi. His descendants at Bhinai in Ajmer have survived into the present age as useful members of society in independent India.

Of the nineteen chiefs of Ajmer virtually all are Rathores descended from Rao Jodha at different stages of the genealogical tree. Most are further descended from the three main chiefs - Bhinai, Masuda and Pisangan. ( The only non-Rathore principality is Sawar a Sisodia). As the progeny of the Rathore clan in Marwar proliferated, these descendants of the junior branches were left with no option but to seek their fortunes further afield from Marwar. Most of them displaced the Parmar and Gaur Rajputs and tribal Bhils who had settled here in the wake of Prithviraj Chauhan. Thereafter, they remained firmly in possession of the new fiefdoms they established. Many of them received recognition from Emperor Akbar and Jehangir for services rendered to the Mughals, legitimizing their position as Tazimi Istimirardars, or hereditary estates held in perpetuity subject to certain feudal liabilities.

After Emperor Akbar's successful campaign against Chittor, he arrived at Ajmer on 6 March, 1568. Bhupati's opportunity to present himself before the Emperor had finally arrived. The Emperor remained in Ajmer for just two days before returning to Delhi. Two years later on 11 March, 1570 he came to Ajmer again, this time on foot for worship at the shrine of the Khwaja and to convey his gratitude for his prayer having been answered with the birth of a son ( Salim – later called Jehangir). On this second occasion also Bhupati was able to present himself before the Emperor. The 'Pothis', historical records of the Masuda principality, mention that "then he touched the feet of the Padishah", which would mean making obeisance in the manner ordained by Mughal court protocol.

The Bahi Bhats of Masuda further record an interesting anecdote. In 1570 'Akbar Shah' and 'Salim Shah' were on a boating excursion, engaged in water sports

only seven years after his first arrival at court that he was able to return to Masuda in 1595. However the Emperor was aware of the need to reward as much as punish and a returning Rajput Chief must do so with no rancour in his heart. An elephant named Sundergaj was gifted to Narsinhdas. In those days an elephant was the equivalent of a grand limousine. He was also decorated with a jewelled sword, doubtless assuaging to some extent the penal trial by fire of the past bloody campaigns.

In 1605 Akbar passed away and the rulers of Rajputana had to deal with the accession of a new emperor Jehangir. In 1613 Jehangir came to Ajmer in the eighth year of his reign. Narsinhdas having learnt his lesson well hastened to Ajmer to pay obeisance to the new emperor. As the records put it 'Padishah Ke Pagan Lagya', he touched the feet of the emperor.

Frequent visits had created a fondness for Ajmer in the imperial reckoning. It was no Kashmir, but had always been renowned for its dry and bracing air. Later in the British period several TB Sanatoria were therefore located here to benefit from the healing qualities of the air. The Ana Sagar and Fai Sagar lakes were also developed by the Mughals adding to its scenic beauty. Akbar had built a pavilion of translucent marble which exists to this day and would sit in it to enjoy the lake view sunsets. Hills of the Aravalli range surrounded the city. The Madar hill, now totally bare, was then deeply forested, inhabited by tigers, panthers and other game. The Mughals loved hunting excursions as a major sport and source of leisure and entertainment. In his autobiography Jehangir records : 'while at Ajmer I visited nine times the mausoleum of the revered Khwaja and went to the lake at Pushkar and the Chashm-i-Noor thirty eight times. I went to hunt tigers 50 times and killed 15 tigers, 1 cheetah, 1 lynx, 53 blue bulls, 33 gazelles, 90 antelopes, 80 boars and 340 water fowl". Ajmer at a reasonable distance from Delhi and Agra was not only frequented for pilgrimage to the shrine but also for leisure and vacation. Jehangir also made Ajmer his base for launching campaigns led by his sons to subdue the recalcitrant Sultans of the Deccan.

It was in January 1616 that Sir Thomas Roe, Ambassador from the court of St. James arrived in Ajmer and was granted his first audience with Jehangir on 10$^{th}$ January that year. The lack of importance given to the visit by the Mughals can be seen from the fact that Jehangir makes no mention of it in his diary. Thus passed the visit of the Ambassador of a country which was to become the colonial masters of the country 250 years later. The first audience was granted somewhat casually, not in a regular Durbar, but in a room over the large gate in the circular fortress which later came to be known as the Magazine, where the British arsenal was stored.

The structure of the fort is circular with living quarters for the Queens, nobles, attendants, stables and imperial baths. At the heart of the open circular court is Akbar's lodge surrounded by gardens. The Lodge is a pavilion like structure made of carved Jodhpur red sandstone with six rooms - modest for an imperial regional headquarters. It was used as a kind of rest house for the emperor during his

**Blonde Lady**

pilgrimages to the Khwaja's tomb, a walking distance from it through the bazaar. The Ajmer chiefs were granted audiences here. Today it is a state museum and a recent Sound and Light show brings alive Roe's presentation of credentials to the emperor.

Thomas Roe's description of the Durbar here, gives us a unique and fascinating insight into the atmosphere and grandeur of the event. He describes the scene as closely resembling an Elizabethan theatre staged for King James. Jehangir was seated in a gallery overlooking the rest, as would a King James viewing theatre. On a platform beneath him stood the nobles, cordoned off in three groups according to rank, much as actors playing a part in theatre. The crowd outside appeared to Roe like a cheering audience. Roe climbed three steps to the platform and was escorted through the ranks of nobles, nodding to each of the three groups in greeting. The last group was of the highest order, consisting of Maharajas, Rajas and Ameers. Where would our Bhaputi or Narsinhdas have been located one wonders?

As intimacy between Roe and Jehangir grew over several durbars and meetings. He was finally invited to a more private and intimate gathering by Jehangir. Roe describes the informal atmosphere of the Ghusal Khana or baths. This enclosure where the emperor enjoyed elaborate royal baths also accommodated a kind of royal drawing room, a private chamber for entertaining nobility. It was a place of evening assembly for pleasure games and drinking parties. Here if the emperor commanded, guests could drink wine. However those with wine already on their breaths could be ordered to be flogged for their presumption. When in good spirits the Emperor would scatter gold and silver almonds for his obsequious nobles to scramble to pick up, much to his amusement. By then the party would have "degenerated into a drunken revel". When Jehangir fell into a drunken stupor, the party was at an end, the lights would be snuffed out at the command of the Empress Noor Jehan and the guests would have to grope their way to the entrance in the dark.

Jot Dans, the Masuda archives containing records and miniature paintings, had several paintings of Englishmen of the period. One of the paintings however depicts a blond lady with a pink hat in three quarters portraiture rather than the traditional profile style of portraiture. The three quarters face depiction was an attempt by local artists at realism and being non traditional was reserved for portraying foreigners. The existence of such a miniature in our Jot Dans is indicative of prurient oriental curiosity about European women. Such interest was no less present in the Emperor himself.

Roe recounts Jehangir's birthday celebrations at the fortress at Ajmer. He was suddenly roused from sleep and commanded to join the Padishah in his 'Ghusal Khana' with the request that he bring along the miniature painting of an English lady which Jehangir was aware he secretly possessed from his spies. The tiny portrait was that of his beloved deceased lady love. Obeying the imperial command, he proceeded to the baths. It was his duty as an Ambassador to please the monarch. He found Jehangir sitting on his throne with decanters of colourful wines on a golden table studded with pearls and precious stones before him. He was first ordered to imbibe wine and then asked to produce the portrait of his lady love which Jehangir in a state of some inebriation admired. He refused to return it, promising that he would treasure it more than his most precious jewels.

The reason for including this colourful anecdote here is both to illustrate the atmospherics of the imperial court from the objective eye of a foreigner and to show why such a portrait became a precious collector's item in our own Jot Dans. Doubtless the incident must have become common knowledge among courtiers, firing the imagination of the Ajmer chiefs. According to some records an English factory, subordinate to the one at Surat existed at Ajmer under one Master Edwards. Tom Coryat the inveterate and eccentric traveller who met Roe at Chittor and another traveller Withingdon visited Ajmer in 1615.

They were known to have close association with local chiefs according to the historian Haribilas Sharda. The portrait of the English lady in our Jot Dans is a reminder of the interaction which would have begun to develop between them and the European world.

In 1623 Narsinhdas passed away having been forty years at the helm as against Bhaputi's twenty. He would have been around sixty, a ripe age for the times when the normal life span brought old age after the fortieth birthday. People rarely survived six decades on account of disease, a strenuous life and frequent warfare. At that reckoning he would have spent some twenty eight years after returning to Masuda, in full possession of his fiefdom with imperial sanction. He had also the good fortune and diplomatic skill to pay obeisance to two great Mughal Emperors. He also had enough time to engage in leisure and the arts as the English lady's portrait testifies and develop his fortress and the affairs of the principality, bequeathing a more settled and prosperous estate to his successors.

# 4

# Vassals of the Mughal Empire

## Jhunjhar Singh (1623 – 1650)

Narsinhdas was more prolific than his predecessor, probably the bonus of a more settled estate. For the record we shall name his seven sons: Jhunjhar, Sabal, Shyam, Roop, Chattar, Durjan and Raj. Jhunjhar succeeded him in 1623.

Five years later upon Jehangir's death, overcoming all manner of intrigue by Empress Noor Jehan to promote her protégé, Shah Jehan succeeded to the throne. Ironically, the same house of Mewar which was finally subdued by Khurram (as Shah Jehan was known before he assumed that title), became the one to give him the tidings of the death of his father.

Mewar had fiercely preserved its independent status until Khurram brought it to heel and finally this last and most prestigious Rajput Kingdom also accepted Mughal suzerainty. Rana Amar Singh did so on the condition that he would not appear in person before the Emperor but would send his son Karan to make the acknowledgement. Jehangir delighted at the capitulation of the last bastion of Rajput resistance had asked his son to be gracious to the vanquished Rana and "treat this illustrious one according to his hearts desire". The bashful and embarrassed Mewar prince arriving at the Mughal court was loaded with gifts and honours from one day to another and made a Mansabdar of the empire. At Khurram's specific urgings Jehangir even allowed him a seat directly to his right, an honour denied even to his senior most nobility. All territories were also restored to Mewar. At court, Karan's younger brother Bheem developed a friendship with Khurram and became his chief advisor. This proximity alarmed Jehangir who was always suspicious of his son. To separate him from Khurram, Bheem was offered Governorship of Gujarat, which he declined.

Later suffering the machinations of Noor Jehan, Khurram became a rebel and received the support of Rajputs on account of his Rajput lineage. Jehangir sought to crush Khurram's revolt. In the battle Bheem was killed and Khurram with the estranged army commander Mahabat Khan sought asylum in Udaipur. Khurram and his family were housed in what is today the Lake Palace. It was built with every conceivable luxury to provide comfort to the renegade prince for the consideration he had shown the House of Mewar at the Mughal court in its hour of discomfiture.

Thus it was that upon Jehangir death the Rana in gratitude for Khurram's friendship sent a band of Rajputs to the south to escort Khurram to Udaipur. Khurram had been sent after being pardoned by Jehangir to Burhanpur, an isolated and inconsequential post. It was at Udaipur that Khurram was first hailed as emperor and assumed the title of Shah Jehan. The Rana was presented a precious ruby and all his territories were restored to him with permission to reconstruct the great fortress of Chittor.

Shah Jehan then proceeded to Ajmer and onwards to the imperial capital Agra with his generals Mahabat Khan and Khan Jehan for the formal investiture ceremony. Asaf Khan his father-in-law awaited him there with clear instructions to put to the sword all likely contenders to the throne. The celebrations at Ajmer en route gave Jhunjhar Singh the opportunity to pay homage to the new Padishah.

The Mughal Empire was at its zenith during the reign of Shah Jehan. Though the son of a Rajput princess of Marwar, he had been entrusted by his grandfather Akbar, to one of his childless wives Rukkiya Begum who brought him up as an orthodox Muslim. He however retained a soft corner for Rajputs as this close association with Mewar shows. His Persian wife Mumtaz Mahal's influence also had the effect of making his somewhat bigoted and a staunch Muslim unlike his father, grandfather and son Dara Shikoh.

At first he sought to avenge himself against the Portuguese at Hoogly for earlier denying him asylum when he was seeking to escape his father's wrath. While Mewar was amply rewarded with the restoration of the territories and allowed to enjoy peace, tranquility and development, the Portuguese base by the same yardstick was totally decimated, thousands being put to the sword, converted or enslaved. Later in 1623 in keeping with Islamic tenets which allowed 'infidels' to worship in existing temples but prohibited the construction of new temples, he ordered the demolition of all temples recently begun. Churches in particular were destroyed and land and buildings given earlier to Jesuits were resumed. In later years under the influence of Dara Shikoh he mellowed and became more tolerant. He did not however take his orthodoxy to extremes and was more statesman than bigot. His army and administration remained full of Hindus.

It was a reign of extraordinary prosperity for the empire, though the populace suffered from his heavy taxation for building the numerous monuments and palaces he commissioned.

A French traveller Tavernier testifies to firm administration of justice and a universal sense of security.

Shah Jehan's demeanour was one of gravity, calm and imperial disdain. As

Thomas Roe puts it "I never saw so settled a countenance ... so constant a gravity, never smiling ... weighed with extreme pride and contempt for all". He wished to project himself from the beginning as imperial and above the ordinary, clothed in the costliest attire, fabulous jewellery and surrounded by the grandest court the world had seen. Unlike Jehangir who would jest and play with his nobles in the Ghusal Khana, Shah Jehan was formal and decorous with total absence of any facetiousness. He remained a perfectionist in all fields. His creation the Taj Mahal truly represented his nature and demeanour - august, grand, magnificent, stately and perfect. It is said that he was greatly responsible for its superb style, finesse and restrained magnificence and aesthetics. He was surrounded at all times by the Persians, whether his wife, nobles or generals and he adopted Persian formalism in court etiquette and protocol. He was also essentially abstemious, afraid of loosing control and appearing drunk.

The fabled Peacock Throne was commissioned in his reign, made of solid gold with fabulous gems at a cost of ten million rupees. Pageants and royal processions were frequently arranged to please and awe the public. No emperor undertook to build as many palaces, fortresses, mosques and mausoleums as Shah Jehan, bleeding the imperial treasury white and putting enormous strain on the populace through exorbitant taxes. The Taj Mahal, Jama Masjid Delhi, Pearl Mosque Agra, the new city of Shahjehanabad at Delhi with its magnificent royal residences, a mosque at Sindh, the Shalimar garden and pavilions in Lahore, palaces at Kabul and Kashmir were all constructed during his reign. Akbar's red sand stone monuments were pulled down and replaced by marble structures. At Ajmer a magnificent palace was built on the Ana Sagar lake side which became his residence during visits, rather than the utilitarian Akbar Lodge. Only the 'Baradari' however stands to remind us of the once opulent palace.

Dwelling on the reign of Shah Jehan in some detail is vital in giving us an idea of the socioeconomic conditions of the times, the architectural splendour and flourishing arts and crafts of the empire which reached a peak during the life and times of Jhunjhar Singh. It would have created an army of artisans, craftsman, architects, masons, miners etc. the length and breadth of the country providing employment and generating wealth, economic development and advancement in technologies and skills.

Doubtless the furious construction activity in Ajmer, Agra, Delhi, Lahore and Udaipur would have had their own flow over effects on the modest court and the citizens of the fiefdom of Masuda as well, particularly as the intercourse between the Mughals and the Rajputs had become the bedrock of empire.

Notable travellers apart from Hawkins and Thomas Roe, like the Frenchman Tavernier, Della Valle and the German Albert Mandelslo, have left behind their written impressions of the country. Mandelslo a former page at the court of the Duke of Holstein journeyed from Surat to Agra through Ahmedabad and back via Lahore. He was impressed by what he saw in a journey of eight months through Mughal India. He found the court of the Governor of Ahmadabad more magnificent than any in Europe. At Agra he speaks of streets that were fine and spacious. Some were vaulted for merchants, traders and shopkeepers. There were different streets for different trades and eighty caravanserais for foreign merchants, three stories high with noble lodgings, stone houses, vaults and stables. There were eight hundred public baths. Outside the city were numerous palaces of Rajas and nobles, the most magnificent being the imperial palace with fortification, moat and drawbridge. He remarks that every nation in the East was represented here in commerce. A Roman missionary father Sebastian Manrique says Agra stretched six miles along the Jamuna with a population of six Lakhs.

We now find numerous English, Portuguese, French, German and Italian travellers, Ambassadors, missionaries, traders and factors roaming freely about the empire in relative security with imperial sanction, interacting with the nobility of the fiefdoms. European factories, storehouses, dwellings and churches were coming up at Surat, Ahmadabad, Agra, Ajmer, Masulipatam, Cambay and Baroda. With the mighty European ships docking in the ports on the east, west and south of the subcontinent, the splendid isolation of India was now coming to an end. Heretofore the influence on art, architecture and technology had come through the passes in the north through Islamic conquerors from Samarkand, Turkey, Persia and Arabia, all oriental. Now began the wave of occidental influences, European culture and Christian values, stirring the melting pot of sub-continental culture to produce yet another metamorphosis. It was an age when the West was breaking out of the chrysalis of its medieval past which was not unlike the static moribund oriental world. It was struggling against the forces of orthodoxy to emerge into a world of science, technology, exploration, innovation and invention in diverse fields from astronomy to physics, chemistry, mathematics and biology, all contributing to the military sciences and the art of warfare. Soon the effects of this explosive catharsis would be felt in the tradition bound and static orient through military, naval and strategic superiority bringing the grand empire of the Mughals to its knees and all mighty kingdoms and fiefdoms of India to heel. Roe's warning that the Mughal Empire could not conceivably be overcome by warfare would soon be proved false. The British Empire would replace the Mughal Empire in barely two centuries.

Returning to Jhunjhar Singh we find that he was despatched in 1631 with Nawab Mahbub Mahabat Khan to quell the rebellion of the Golcha Sultan. Many of his companions died in the battle. The archives mention that he was sorry to lose his favourite stallion Mayurdhwaj in the battle. He also suffered many wounds on his head, legs and chest. The Padishah always mindful of rewarding bravery gave him 'Niwajis', gifts and honours. He was given the Parganah of Soba. Later in recognition of his participation in several campaigns throughout his life, he was gifted a horse called Arampanna, a Siropao (royal robes), Sarpech ( turban broach), a pearl necklace and a sword and sent home.

Jhunjhar died in 1650 after a rule of twenty seven years, leaving behind seven sons. Ajab, Balbadhra, Kan, Kusha, Mokham, Udai and Gopaldas. Till his time fragmentation of the estate was avoided on the principle of primogeniture wherein the eldest son was deemed the 'Patvi' as heir and the others were treated as 'Thatwis' or those who had to carve out their own fortunes on the saddle left largely to their own devises. They rarely came to partake in parental inheritance. However, this was about to change.

**Ajab Singh**

# 5

# Faujdar of Ajmer

## Ajab Singh (1650 - 1684)

In a span of about ninety years, three generations had passed since Bhupati's arrival at Masuda from Merta. Shah Jehan was still on the Peacock Throne and it was the Golden Age of the Mughal Empire. The arts flourished and artisans of every description were in great demand at the imperial capital and the provincial kingdoms and fiefdoms. Architecture had reached a level of perfection with the completion of the Taj Mahal, Itmad-ud-daulah's tomb and Fatehpur Sikri. At Amber and elsewhere palaces and halls of audience were replicating Mughal splendour in Rajputana. Music, dance and poetry were a feature of court activity. European factories had sprung up at the seaports and in the interior. Trade and commence were booming. There was administrative order, stability and security. Foreigners were welcomed, given protection and allowed to roam the empire.

It is evident from the sudden abundance of mid seventeenth century miniature paintings in the Masuda 'Jot Dans' that the principality of Masuda had not remained unaffected by these developments. Being so close to Ajmer, the Mughal Suba headquarters of Rajputana, the influences were available at first hand. The Chiefs of Masuda furthermore had travelled across the country in campaigns and battles, shoulder to shoulder with Maharajas, Nawabs and Persian and Turkish generals. They had been received in audience by the Emperors, experienced the splendour of the imperial court and been suitably rewarded with gifts, titles and Sanads. They were now a part of the Mughal gentry.

The availability of the paintings is invaluable as source material on the history of the times. In some ways they surpass in significance the written records of the Bahikhatas and the bardic couplets handed down by word of mouth from generation to generation. It is only through the paintings that one can picture the personality, attire, way of life, culture and habits of the feudal order. It is as if we have progressed from the radio to television. The portraiture of the chiefs tells us more than any poem or record could. For the first time the chiefs commissioned their portraits, giving a face and personality to a name.

The 'Jot Dans' have an abundance of miniature paintings of the highest quality from the middle of the seventeenth century on every conceivable subject. Paintings for instance of the Rag Mala series show that the Masuda court was now enjoying sophisticated forms of classical music. There are paintings of dancers, bathing beauties, gods and goddesses, themes from the Puranas and epics, hunts, elephant fights, processions, court scenes, even portraits of the ladies of the distant Mughal and Deccan courts. The array of themes is indicative of a cultural explosion, raising self esteem and confidence in the tiny principality, which defies the imagination. They reveal not only the evolution of the feudal order from a band of adventurers seeking their fortunes in a dark and dismal no-mans-land infested by roving bandits, to an elite nobility now well entrenched in a prosperous fiefdom engaged in refined and leisurely pursuits, promoting and patronizing art, culture and aesthetics within a mere century of arrival.

The paintings are evidence not only of a highly successful local promotion of the arts but also of the Chiefs acquiring works of art on their travels, albeit on warlike campaigns to Malwa, Gujarat and further afield at the imperial capital and beyond to the Deccan. Numerous miniature paintings of the Deccan, Mughal and Indo-Persian Schools stand testimony to this. These were no mere hardy warriors who only suffered and inflicted deadly wounds in bloody wars but people with varied interests embracing the fine arts. Evidently they were men with acute aesthetic sensibilities beyond their martial and heroic capabilities. They were in fact travellers and tourists albeit with sword in hand.

What we see happening in the tiny principality of Masuda is indeed symptomatic of similar upsurges of art and literature across Rajputana, the evidence of a fusion of Rajput heroism and chivalry and genius for romance and poetry with the Mughal eclecticism and craving for excellence in fine arts, architecture and literature derived from India, Central Asia, Arabia, Turkey and Persia. Thenceforth, miniature paintings, palace murals, classical music, dance, architecture, astrology and the occult spread across the land, finding ready patrons in the macrocosm of the Mughal Empire and new found enthusiasts in the microcosm of the feudal order of Rajputana.

Ajab Singh's portrait is in the style of the Ajmer School of miniature paintings. Each of the schools of painting developed their own distinctive genre, paramount being Ajmer, Kishangarh, Jodhpur, Jaipur, Bundi, Sirohi, Deogarh, Kota, Kangra, Basholi, Deccan and Mughal. The Ajmer school is closest in style to that of the Mughal School on account of the direct influence of the Mughals on the Ajmer Suba Headquarters. Ajab Singh's portrait is no run of the mill instant portraiture. It is an exquisite work of art which could only have been painted by an artist of the highest calibre trained in the finest traditions of the great Mughal School of painting. (For this reason it has been adopted as the cover page of the book)

The interactions with the Mughal court during campaigns would have put the Chiefs of Masuda in touch with artists and craftsmen of the Mughal capital and enabled him to commission a portrait of such excellence. Was the painter a visitor lured at great expense to Masuda for the assignment? Did the subject pose for the portrait at Delhi or Agra during a visit, or was the court of the little fiefdom now enriched by painters, musicians, dancers, craftsman, bards and jesters, taking the inspiration from Akbar's nine gems the 'Nav Ratna' of the imperial court? Looking at the painting these questions flood the mind.

The portrait of Ajab Singh shows a stout, stately prince attired in Mughal headgear and tunic sitting on his cushions and pillows, the traditional 'Gadi-Mora' of a feudal chief, being offered a beetle leaf, the 'Pan', by a Rajput lady of exquisite beauty and proportions. Ajab's headgear is white to match the white muslin of the tunic and laced with gold to match the sash around his waist. It is to be noted that the tunic, known as the 'Angarkha', is made of the finest white translucent muslin and is in the haute couture of Mughal fashions of the day. Thus from neck to shoulder line, the Angarkha is of a darker, plum hue running horizontally across half the chest. The Pantaloon visible under the muslin tunic is blue candy-striped and held in place by a golden brocaded sash tightly wound round his ample waist.

The Angarkha is tied to his left. That is the only give away that he is not a Mughal but a Rajput. The Mughal tunic would have been tied to the right. A 'Katar' is tucked into his sash on one side. It is exquisitely enameled. His hand is extended to receive the 'Pan'. He is seated on a Persian carpet with several flagons of wine and barbequed corn, snacks and something like popcorn in a container resting beside him. The sword lies ceremonially on one side. The lady is in a gold skirt clinging to her form, embroidered with flowers. She wears a tight fitting red blouse or 'Choli' just covering the breasts in Rajasthani style. Her hair is loose and apparently wet with one curling strand falling on one side. She is looking him in the eye, doe like. His features are well defined and realistic in true early Mughal miniature style, without the poetic exaggeration one sees in later Marwar or Kishengarh paintings.

He has small eyes, a fine nose and a moustache curving downwards in the Mughal style, over pursed lips. The painting is so realistic that the face shows dark shadows where his shaved beard could grow. He is sitting on a marble open pavilion, the 'Chabutra' and against the apple green dusk, after sunset, a pale moon is visible up high, with stars growing brighter as the sky turns dark at the zenith. There remains no doubt in ones mind how Ajab Singh would have looked in real life. The portraiture is perfect, almost European Renaissance in its realism. He is handsome and she is so pretty. They look pleased with themselves. We begin to realize how extraordinarily valuable the painting is as source material for our narrative.

Soon after Ajab Singh's accession, the Governor of Ajmer, Subedar Hafiz Nazir Shah commanded him to undertake a campaign to curb the depredations of Umoji Sindhal, a notorious marauder who had abducted sixteen wealthy merchants, carrying them away to his Sindhalvati region near Bhadrajun. Ajab Singh told the Governor that the task was an arduous one involving passage through deep forest tracts and over mountains, but assured him that he would undertake it. Ajab Singh then summoned his 'Zami Zamayat' of Zamindars, the notable landowners, farmers and soldiering classes. A large force of horsemen was mustered and he marched at their head to Singhalvati. He scouted out the secret approaches to Umoji's base and encircled it from two flanks. After a furious battle Umoji was captured and killed and the sixteen Seths were released. Ajab Singh then proceeded to plunder the area, bringing back camel and horse loads of wealth which helped him develop his estate. The Subedar, on his victorious return, sent a procession of camels, horses, chariots and an elephant to receive him with honours. The episode was duly reported to the Emperor with high recommendations. In recognition for his consistent support for the Subedar's campaigns he was given the prestigious post of Faujdar (commander) of Ajmer with a daily honorarium called 'Thal-Kharch' (daily allowance) of 25 dinars. He was also given complete charge of the region populated by the Mer ( also known as Merat ) tribe, called Merwara.

The Mer tribes were notoriously independent minded and given to raiding neighbouring territories for loot. The imperial powers, whether Mughal or later the British were always concerned to keep them in check for the security of the citizenry of the region and for the safe passage of caravans to promote trade and commerce. Ajab Singh now required them to pay Chauth or a quarter of their produce to him. They were also to send contingents to battle when the need arose. The Mers are a unique tribal entity adopting both Hindu and Islamic customs with uncertainly about their actual faith. A large proportion had however converted to Islam. The areas they inhabited were in the vicinity of Masuda and today form part of the Assembly Constituency. Ajab Singh cultivated such good relation with them that even today three centuries later their loyalty towards Masuda Chiefs had remained unshaken. They voted en masse for a descendant of Ajab Singh seeking elections from the constituency in democratic India.

Let us now turn to the momentous developments that were taking place at the heart of the Empire. By 1655 Shah Jehan had virtually fragmented the empire by devolving power upon his four sons to quell their rampant jealousies and buy himself a life of greater ease and peace. Aurangzeb the trouble maker had been consigned to the south as Governor of the Deccan and was busy trying to subdue the Adil Shahi rule at Bijapur, the Kutub Shahis of Golkunda and the Nizam Shahis of Ahmednagar. Murad Baksh was sent west as Governor of Gujarat while Shuja was despatched east as Governor of Bengal. Dara Shikoh, the favourite son, though nominally Governor of Kabul & Kandhar in the North, had stationed himself at Delhi and Agra close to the Emperor. Each was building his army for the inevitable battle for succession.

In 1657 the rumour spread of serious illness and imminent death of Shah Jehan, though he was to survive for another decade till 1667. The first to revolt was Shuja who even struck coins in his name as emperor and marched upon Agra to claim the throne. Dara sent the imperial army against him under Mirja Raja Jai Singh of Amber. Shuja was vanquished at Banares and fled. Next Dara turned to deal with Murad.

It is at this time that Ajab Singh proceeded to Agra ostensibly to pay homage to the Emperor but in fact to learn at first hand about developments in the imperial capital following reports of the Emperor approaching demise. Dara had ordered Maharaja Jaswant Singh of Jodhpur to lead the army against Murad who was located at Ujjain. Ajab Singh was commanded to join Jaswant's forces in the campaign. Jaswant was also appointed Governor of Malwa and raised in his Mansab rank. The commander of the imperial forces, Qasim Khan however proved treacherous and secretly connived with Murad. Meanwhile Aurangzeb pooled his resources to form a joint front with Murad against the imperial force sent by Dara. The imperial forces which were to be the backbone of the campaign did not engage, standing aloof when Jaswant's forces attacked Murad's army. The Rajputs fought bravely but without the support of the imperial forces were totally decimated. Of their eight thousand men all but six hundred were massacred. Maharaja Jaswant suffered serious personal wounds and was forced to withdraw to Marwar with his rump. The Masuda Bahikhatas mention that among those killed were forty four soldiers accompanying Ajab Singh who himself suffering twenty two wounds. Like the Maharaja, after the rout, Ajab Singh also retreated and hastened home with his surviving forces. Jaswant Singh on return to Jodhpur faced his wife's scorn. She is reported to have shut the palace gates in order not to welcome a vanquished warrior. We have no knowledge from the 'Rani Mangas', Queen's Annals of Masuda, whether Ajab Singh received a similar cool reception.

Dara now prepared to face the combined victorious forces of Murad and Aurangzeb. He put together an impressive army of a hundred thousand horse, twenty thousand infantry and eighty artillery pieces. Yet he was destined to lose. Just as Murad's armies were losing ground under a Rajput charge and the battle was turning against Aurangzeb, Dara committed the fatal error of dismounting from his elephant, when his Howdah was hit by a cannon ball. He was advised by one of his generals in league with the enemy to dismount to safety. Meanwhile Murad and Aurangzeb could be seen firmly installed on their elephants. Dara's army, close to victory, took the vacant Howdah as a sign of capitulation of their chief and began a sudden retreat, fleeing in panic. Aurangzeb emerged victorious. Through another stratagem the guileful Aurangzeb had his brother Murad treacherously put to death, eliminating yet one more contender. Shah Jehan was then made a virtual prisoner and Aurangzeb mounted the Peacock Throne.

Dara meanwhile had retreated to Ajmer. Aurangzeb pursued the last challenger to the throne by forced marches day and night and in 1657 Ajmer witnessed the great battle. Mirza Raja Jai Singh the vanquisher of Shuja, sensitive to the changing tide of events, changed sides and pledged support for the victor Aurangzeb. He warned Jaswant Singh to refrain from supporting Dara. In his letter to Jaswant Singh, who had already advanced to join Dara, Jai Singh assured him of Aurangzeb's pardon and restoration of all honours if he immediately transferred loyalty to Aurangzeb. If he failed to do so he was warned that he would not be spared. Jaswant was thus persuaded to revoke his pledge and despite entreaties through Dara's son, changed sides deserting Dara.

Dara deployed his artillery all around the hills of Ajmer and a vigorous battle was fought for four days. The hills resounded with the thunder of gunfire and the ground shook with the charge of cavalry and infantry. Ajmer had never experienced so much tumult. Despite the charge of Mirja Raja Jai Singh from the front and Raja Ram Rup of Jammu at the near, Dara was still at no real disadvantage militarily. But yet again before the battle had become decisive he lost his nerve and took flight with his family. Finally he was captured and paraded in disgrace in torn garments on a small and sickly elephant across Delhi. When the populace showed universal revulsion and sympathy and there were signs of a popular uprising at this atrocity, Dara was summarily imprisoned and executed.

Dara was a scholar and a mystic, popular among the masses and famed for his tolerance towards Hindus, a natural successor to the ideals and precepts of his great ancestor Akbar. He had studied the Talmud, the New Testament, the Upanishads, and Sufi thought and sought to find common ground between religions. He wrote a book 'Majmuhat Al Bahrein' the confluence of two oceans, drawing parallels in the thought of Islam and Hinduism. He undertook translations from the Upanishads from Sanskrit to Persian and believed they were the source of monotheistic thought, not at variance with the Holy Koran. He disliked the Muslim clergy and is quoted as having said 'paradise is where no mullah exists'. Unfortunately he was also disdainful of the Amirs, the Persian, Afghan and Turkish nobility and preferred the company of Hindu mendicants, Brahmins and mystics and dreamt of renouncing the world. Had such a Mughal ascended the throne, the course of Indian history may have been dramatically different. But despite being Shah Jehan's favourite son and his gracious character and attainments, the establishment opposed him, believing that his succession would not only be a threat to Islam but also to their own careers and prospects.

The story of his final months on the run as a fugitive from pillar to post, pursued even by the Mirza Raja of Amber and Maharaja Jaswant Singh and finally being betrayed while escaping to Kabul by the very Pathan chief whose life he had spared from imperial wrath, showed that when out of power the whole world turned against you. The Pathan chief's betrayal thus culminated tragically in his captivity. His pleadings with Aurangzeb that he be spared as he had no real ambitions and would be content to retire as a humble scholar and even pray for Auranzeb's wellbeing was received with utter scorn and he was beheaded. He was again paraded, this time as a headless torso through the capital city to the shock and horror of the voiceless populace, while his estranged sister Roshanara threw a feast to celebrate his murder. Aurangzeb is also said to have sent the severed head of the favourite son on a covered platter to Shah Jehan, reminding him that he too had dealt ruthlessly with his brothers.

The manner in which this paragon of virtue was betrayed, hounded, executed and thereafter paraded headless, must be reckoned as the most barbaric, brutal and tragic episodes in Indian history. What followed was a reign of unmitigated bigotry and untold privations inflicted on the Hindu masses which eventually sealed the fate of the Mughal Empire. It is no wonder and perhaps poetic justice that not one Mughal descendent has survived into the present age.

The Ajmer Chiefs taking the cue from Raja Jai Singh of Amber and Maharaja Jaswant Singh of Jodhpur remained aloof from the events and by that virtue have indeed survived to this day to tell a tale.

It appears that Ajab Singh's joining the imperial forces at Dara Shikoh's bidding against Murad and Aurangzeb was not held against him even as Jai Singh's earlier campaign against Shuja at Dara's orders was not. Ajab Singh's decision to remain aloof rather than join forces in defence of Dara following Jaswant Singh's example, appears to have decided Aurangzeb in favour of pardoning their earlier campaigns against Murad and not interpreted as being specifically directed against him.

In 1661 while Ajab Singh was rendering service to the Padshah, Raja Udai Bhan of the neighbouring fief of Bhinai raided Masuda and occupied it. Aurangzeb ordered that an expedition be sent to expel the Raja and the fief of Masuda was thereby restored to Ajab. From this it is evident that Ajab had managed to win over the confidence of the new Emperor and his earlier association with Dara had been forgotten or forgiven.

In 1684 Ajab Singh was treacherously murdered at Pahi by one Udawat Kaniram. The Pahi Thakur then fled to Jaipur. Thus despite an extraordinarily successful career, the promotion of the arts within the estate and ushering in stability and economic progress for the fiefdom and being a recipient of honours from the Empire he met a premature and tragic end after a rule of thirty four years.

This should come as no surprise, considering that it was the order of the day. Even at the highest level, Dara Shikoh had met a similar fate, being brutally put to death. Medieval India was an Hobbesonian world where the life of a person tended to be nasty, brutish and short. In fact this was a universal feature of the medieval era, where might alone was right, the end justifying the means and all manner of subterfuge, betrayal, warfare and assassinations were sanctioned for achieving personal goals, particularly when there was a throne in question. The epic Mahabharat was a dark reminder that kith and kin were the first adversary and every intrigue and deceit was justified for attaining the seat of power and self aggrandizement. There were no qualms, whether it was an Aurangzeb decapitating his brother Dara or then an Elizabeth beheading her sister Mary Stuart. Both belonged to the same order of ruthlessness and cold blooded calculations in the pursuit of power.

There were no well established hereditary rights either, from the lowest to the highest levels of society, indeed no charter of fundamental rights existed and princes suffered the same insecurity as the common man, in the absence of a rule of law or a stable nation state. With every succeeding generation and change in the incumbency of Empire, estates, fiefs, land, buildings, tenancies, movable and immovable wealth could all be confiscated and resumed to the state and their restoration to successors and claimants remained at the mercy and pleasure of the ruling monarch and ultimately the supreme power in the shape of the emperor. In such circumstances the fact that the Ajmer Chiefs survived generation after generation retaining control over their fiefs despite all odds must be regarded as a Machiavellian achievement and a tribute to their diplomatic and martial genius.

# 6

# Rajput Alienation

## Maun Singh (1684 – 1700)

Ajab Singh had six sons. Under the Mughals the law of primogeniture became modified and younger brothers were not deprived of their inheritance but allowed a limited share of the estate for their maintenance. As Thakurs they were no longer required to fend for themselves without any support from the principality. For four generations the estate had remained un-fragmented, under the strict code of primogeniture, but thereafter, sub-divisions became frequent. The sub-divisions however did not involve an equal partition of the estate among the progeny of the ruler, as was current in the Shekhawati region of Jaipur. The principle was not equal partition but a limited arrangement for providing maintenance. A failure to produce heirs or to pay dues and discharge responsibilities towards the fief lord could entail annexation. Thus one or more village was apportioned to the 'Thatvis' with the area immediately appurtenant to it as a Jagir with hereditary rights for progeny. The 'Thatvis' then proceeded to build their own fortresses and dwellings within it and farm the lands appurtenant to it. They acquired farms, collected revenues from peasants and taxes from merchants in their allotted villages and provided support to the 'Patvi', the ruler of the fief, militarily as and when required. They came to be termed the 'Bhayat' or extended brotherhood of the ruler of the principality and were termed Thakurs. When the main line of the 'Patvis' failed to produce heirs, the closest link in the lineage was traced to one of these branches. The 'Bhayat' thus became the source for perpetuating dynastic succession.

As 'Patvi' or eldest, Maun Singh succeeded as the ruler of Masuda while his brothers received 'Thikanas' for maintenance. Thus Kaiser Singh received the village of Sathana, Lamba and Nagar, Bakht Singh received Kesarpura, Lalawas, Akrol and Ramgarh, Jaskaran received Sikhrani, Girdardas received Jamola and Amar Singh received Khuntia. In later generations there were further subdivisions of the Thikanas themselves and at Independence for instance those which emerged

**Maun Singh**

within the major principality of Masuda were: Shergarh, Sathana, Lamba, Nagar, Kesarpura, Lalawas, Ramgarh and Sikhrani, each with its fort or 'Gad' and Thakur.

It then became the practice of the 'Bhayat' or brotherhood, to place the eldest on the 'Patvi Pat', the throne and offer 'Nazar', the ceremonial token of allegiance and 'Nichrawal', the monetary offering of subservience.

In British times it was only after receiving a report of the completion of this exercise that a representative of the A.G.G. Rajputana and the Chief Commissioner Ajmer would arrive at the Durbar (court) of the fiefdom and formally read out the letter of recognition in the name of H.E. the Viceroy on behalf of the Britannic Majesty. The Mughal modification of the law of primogeniture was essentially reversed during the times of the British Raj and further fragmentations were discouraged.

Maun Singh after his installation summoned his 'Jami-Jamayat', the above Jagirdars, Muajidars, Bhumias etc. different categories of share holders in the fief, and consulted his brothers regarding the action to be taken to avenge the murder of their father Ajab Singh. It appears that the murder was provoked by some action taken by Ajab in his capacity as Faujdar of Ajmer in pursuance of some imperial Mughal mandate. The Thakur of Pahi who had fled after the dire deed, was traced out and the fortress in which he had taken sanctuary was attacked. The walls were scaled by ladders and the gates were blown open. Maun Singh's forces entered with general slaughter and plunder and the Thakur of Pahi was killed by Maun Singh, thus avenging his father's murder to the satisfaction of the brotherhood.

The Jot-dans have a miniature painting of Maun Singh as well, a devoted son bent on avenging his father's assassination. It appears to have been painted by the same artist who created the portrait of Ajab Singh, as the style is identical. This too is a painting superbly executed in the Mughal Ajmer style. It shows Maun Singh in typical Mughal attire of white muslin, in two tones, again tied to the left as befitted a Rajput as against a Mughal. His Angarkha is olive from neck to shoulder and the rest white, with headgear of gold and crimson. The headgear has undergone some modification and is not as typically Mughal as was Ajab Singh's, though it is pretty close. He resembles his father with small eyes, a fine aquiline nose, drooping moustache in the Mughal style and stylish side burns. His pantaloons visible under the muslin tunic is also candy-striped with maroon bands. There is a gold sash around the girdle. He appears to be in his early twenties and is exceedingly handsome, fair and slim. He is seated on a rearing white dappled horse with grey legs, the ends of which are hennaed. The horse has been superbly executed in the best traditions of a Mughal painting. Maun Singh is seated armed with a gilded Katar, sword and a quiver full of arrows.

By the time of Maun Singh's succession the bonhomie in relations between the Rajputs and the Mughals had evaporated. Aurangzeb had deliberately taken step after step to bruise and wreck the once intimate relations, failing to realize that the loss of Rajput support would have serious adverse consequences for the integrity of the Empire. Relations which had been built so assiduously by Akbar,

Jehangir and Shah Jehan through extending honours, privileges, marital alliances and the display of utmost consideration towards religious sensitivities of their collaborators, were now in tatters in the wake of Aurangzeb's bigoted policies. His predecessors had fully realized that for the Rajput nothing was more important than his honour, prestige, pride, dignity and faith. Their support was deemed invaluable because they were the best fighting forces of the land and their heroism, sincerity and loyalty were unmatched, serving to counterbalance the intrigues, treachery and duplicity of the Persian, Turkish and Afghan nobility.

Aurangzeb was not unaware of the assets which the Rajputs represented but his bigoted convictions brooked no compromise. He also knew that Rajput loyalties towards Akbar, Jehangir and Shah Jehan stemmed from the fact that their wives or mothers were Rajput and they regarded the Mughals therefore as kin, while his mother Mumtaj was a Persian. He had sought to remedy this by himself marrying a Rajput lady. Some historians hold that his sons Mohammad and Muazzim and a daughter were born of her. But this did not have any real effect on him in moderating the bigoted policy he embarked upon. According to some historians he did not even care if his Rajput wife worshipped idols in her apartments as he didn't think this mattered. For him women had no souls worth redeeming.

Next came the hated Jazia tax against the Hindus re-imposed throughout the empire.

After the death of Jaswant Singh, rousing himself to the heights of bigotry he annexed Marwar and sought unsuccessfully to take his posthumous sons hostage with the intention of converting them and later installing on Marwar a Muslim Maharaja. The Rathores were appalled and under Durga Das rose in rebellion. He then marched to Ajmer to suppress the revolt when he found that Mewar had also joined the rebels. Mewar was also ravaged. Thousand of Hindus rose in revolt in Mewat but were slain and the uprising crushed ruthlessly.

Except for Jaipur and the east of Rajputana, the rest reverberated in revolt till the end of his reign. The Rajputs never again joined his armies in the Mughal campaigns in the Deccan. Aurangzeb fought alone in the South without his 'right arm'. The subjugation of the Shia kingdoms of Bijapur and Golkunda and imprisonment of their Sultans actually helped the Marathas in filling the vacuum created as Mughal rule could never fully establish itself in place of the Deccan Sultans, without the vital support of the Rajputs.

While the Rajputs of Marwar and Mewar no longer joined the Mughal forces under Aurangzeb on his campaigns, Jaipur reluctantly continued the association for a while. In fact the young Raja of Jaipur, Jai Singh-II presented himself at the Mughal court when he was barely twelve and his witty repartees impressed the octogenarian Aurangzeb so much that he conferred the honorific of Sawai (greater than one – a one and a quarter's worth), which future rulers of Jaipur continued to prefix to their name. The young Raja later also engaged in campaigns in the Deccan. He was the genius who founded the city of Jaipur with its wide boulevards and the astrological wonders of the Jantar Mantar observatories in Jaipur and elsewhere. The Chiefs of Ajmer being close to the Suba Headquarters could also not act with bravado in daring to offend or challenge the Mughal might and continued with their policy of appeasement and discreet engagement, much the same as they had done in refraining from throwing in their lot with the beloved Dara Shikoh's setting star.

Thus in 1700 Maun Singh went to Delhi to offer his services to Emperor Aurangzeb. As was the custom he was immediately commanded to set off with Mathura Das and an imperial army to Muzaffargarh in Punjab. The fort was placed under siege and its walls were scaled with ladders. After a bitter fight the gates were broken open with the force of elephants. Alas, Maun Singh was killed in the fighting inside the fort though the imperial army returned victorious. Aurangzeb who was busy in the Deccan failed to acknowledge, compensate or decorate the brave hero who laid his life for the empire. Unlike the past when Mughal emperors took great pains to acknowledge bravery by conferring honours, gifts and jagirs, the practice to reward such sacrifice of life and limb had fallen into abeyance with Aurangzeb.

Maun Singh's rule over Masuda lasted for only sixteen years before he was killed in battle in the service of the Empire. No wonder he looks so young in the portrait. It is if he is riding into war on his last campaign.

**Sultan Singh**

# 7

# Empire in Retreat

## Sultan Singh (1700 - 1713)

Sultan Singh was only a youth when he succeeded to the Gaddi. The Mughal Empire was territorially at its zenith with the subjugation of the Deccan Sultans by the octogenarian Aurangzeb. No Mughal had commanded an area larger than did Augangzeb with his stern will and iron grip on the affairs of the empire. But on his death in 1707 it began crumbling and in five years it had all but disappeared. After a brief war of succession, Muazzam the eldest ascended the throne as Bahadur Shah. The empire was in chaos The Marathas had risen in the Deccan, the Rajputs were in revolt, the Sikhs rose suddenly to ravage the Punjab and avenge the deaths of their Gurus, the Jats were up in arm at Agra and the English had now appeared on the scene as new contenders for power. The Governors of the Mughals had become independent in all but name. The Nawabs of Oudh, Bengal and Carnatak and the Nizam of Hyderabad became independent monarchs while nominally acknowledging the authority of the emperor.

After Aurangzeb's death, Marwar, Mewar and Jaipur met to plan the takeover of Delhi. To cement their ties, Mewar's Rana gave his daughter in marriage to Marwar's Ajit Singh who in turn gave his daughter in marriage to Raja Jai Singh of Amber. In 1709 Maharaja Ajit Singh of Marwar, with new found confidence attacked the imperial stronghold at Ajmer. Then he proceeded to punish the chiefs of the Ajmer fiefdoms one after another for their pro-imperial inclinations and failure to support the bid for power by the big three. The chiefs of Deogam, Baghera, Rupgarh, Pisangan, Junia and Kishengarh were made to flee and their fiefs were overrun. However, Masuda was not attacked on account of a Mer apprising in the region. Bhinai and Kharwa were also left alone. The chiefs of Ajmer were perplexed at these developments. They felt that their allegiance to the empire of the 'Dilliwalas' was no more than a matter of expediency and not directed in any way against Marwar. The punitive action against them they felt was therefore unwarranted.

The Ajmer chiefs informed Bahadur Shah of these developments when he was moving south to settle issues in the Deccan. Bahadur Shah turned back arriving in Ajmer in 1710. Sultan Singh availed of the opportunity to present himself before the Padishah at Dandwa same sixty miles from Ajmer and succeeded in obtaining a Sanad from the Emperor in that year. He was commanded to prevent the Mer tribes of Masuda from joining forces with Marwar or Mewar. However, before Bahadur Shah could take any punitive action against the big three, the sudden revolt of the Sikhs left him with no choice but to appease the Rajputs. Jaipur's ruler was reinstated and Ajit Singh was conferred with the title of Maharaja and appointed Subedar of Ahmedabad. Bahadur Shah had made a valiant effort to stem the rot affecting the Mughal Empire by first releasing Sahu in the hope that the Marathas would embroil themselves in an internecine struggle of rival claimants, coming to terms with the Rajputs, restoring them to their positions as under Akbar's reign and driving the Sikhs back into the hills. But before he could do more he died in 1712.

The Mertia Jagmalots of Masuda and other feudatory chiefs had for a century and half enjoyed a fairly settled existence under the protective Mughal umbrella of the Suba headquarters at Ajmer. The only requirement was to provide forces for the imperial army whenever required. The estate remained secure, their dynastic succession assured and their legitimacy acknowledged with grants of Sanads. In a word they had immunity against the ambitions of the regional overlords. The Empire was well administered with elaborate and well defined rules about obligations and duties to be rendered in return for acknowledgement of their rights and privileges as chiefs. There was no interference in their rule over the fiefdoms. Thus they were not subject to the whims and fancies of the overlords of Marwar, Mewar or Jaipur unlike the fiefs under their rulers. The rule under the Maharajas was more erratic and less rational than that of the Empire. With the decline of the Empire the Ajmer Chiefs became wary of the territorial ambitions of the big three. The regional overlords now wished to bring the Ajmer region under their dominion. Mewar had already tried during Aurangzeb's rule to strike a secret deal with his son Azam to incorporate several Parganas of Ajmer including Masuda within Mewar. Ajit Singh also wished to extend his overlordship beyond Merta to the Ajmer region and refused to acknowledge the Sanads granted by the Mughals to the Ajmer chiefs. They suddenly found themselves vulnerable and threatened by the expansionist ambitions of their kinsmen from Mewar, Marwar and Jaipur.

Sultan Singh's problems arising from the growing instability within Rajasthan and the declining authority of the imperial court were further exacerbated by the uprising of the Mer tribes in Masuda and neighbouring Merwara. The Mughals it will be recalled had time and again charged the fiefdom of Masuda with the task of maintaining the stability of Merwara by keeping the tribes in check. Ajab Singh had succeeded admirably in befriending them but later there was growing discontent and unrest.

The Mers are a proud independent minded aboriginal group who claim descent from Prithviraj Chauhan. Essentially they are hill folk who inhabit the Aravalli range of hills between Kishengarh and Ajmer known as Merwara. Their way of life, combines elements both from Hindu and Muslim traditions. A large proportion of them had been converted to Islam. After Dara Shikoh's final defeat at Ajmer he had sought to flee north from Ajmer. The Mers had pursued and looted the baggage train carrying personal effects and valuables of the fallen Mughal leaving him more or less destitute. To pillage the caravan of a Mughal, even one who was disempowered in retreat and in disgrace, was an impudent act and an effrontery for the established order to take lightly. Later Aurangzeb's own son Akbar fleeing after a failed rebellion, supported by Jodhpur, suffered the same fate, being dispossessed of his valuables by the Mer brigands. Agents of the Maharaja of Marwar had then forced the Mers to disgorge the booty. Durga Das had led the campaign to secure their protégé's jewellery. This had enraged the Mers who felt entitled to their loot. They were now intolerant of any further inroads into their territory by Rajput chiefs. The neighboring chieftain of Badnore was already fighting the Mers at Khan Athoon.

Sultan Singh had been charged by Bahadur Shah to keep the tribes in check lest they threw in their lot with either Mewar or Marwar against the Mughals. The Mers were already enraged by the actions of Durga Das and the Badnore chief. Sultan Singh should have realized that intervention at this juncture could prove suicidal. His campaign at the Mughal behest to control them proved to be the last straw and they rebelled. Sultan Singh in view of his inexperience and youth failed to grasp their mood and a furious battle ensued. He was slain in the battle together with several brothers, nobles and henchmen. It was an unmitigated disaster with scores of Rajputs killed and wounded. The tragedy was further compounded when Sultan Singh's wife Rani Chundawatji performed Sati at Masuda with his mortal remains. A pavilion marks the spot, in an enclosure of dynastic cenotaphs called Mahasati Bagh, in honour of her memory. Family members visit the enclosure and make flower offerings at the site to this day.

Fortunately the 'Jot Dans' have a single portrait of Sultan Singh. It shows a handsome youth astride a beautiful chestnut, holding a lance and armed with 'Katar' and sword. He has a halo around his head indicating martyrdom in war. The headgear of gold is essentially Mughal with slight modifications of a loop of cloth tucked in at the back. There is a little down on his upper lip, otherwise it appears that he has yet to grow facial hair. The horse is magnificently executed but with the exaggerations of poetic license of the artist. The realism and precision of his father's Mughal horse are no longer in evidence. The Mughal influence has waned with the fall of the Empire and in its place the influence of Marwar is apparent, particularly in the execution of the horse. Yet this is not a typical work of the Marwar School. The refined and delicate attention to detail in the execution of Sultan Singh's face and the features of the horse are still in the realms of Mughal realism and mark the painting as belonging to the post Mughal phase of the Ajmer

School of paintings. Evidently the execution of this superb work of art, conceived like a poignant poem with fluid lines, graceful movements and postures of horse and man, exquisite but not overbearing detail, indicate that the artist from Delhi, or at least his descendents were still active at the Masuda court and had not lost any of the creative skills of an earlier period. Thus the brave youthful prince has been immortalized by this portrait, making the halo a tragic reminder of his martyrdom. The pavilion at Masuda also commemorates his wife's sacrifice of her life, holding him in her grieving arms as the flames of the funeral pyre would have lept up to consume them.

We find that in five generations, two chiefs were assassinated and two more perished in battle. The life of the chiefs of Rajputana remained nasty, brutish and short. Holding a fief was no exercise in leisure, romance or dalliance. It required at all times, uncommon courage, readiness for adversity and battle and willingness to sacrifice life and limb, in the hope that future generations would survive and prosper. These medieval chiefs were all heroes, no less than their classical counterparts of Greece and Rome.

# 8

# Ajmer - Bone of Contention

## Jai Singh (1713-1761)

Sultan Singh when he was slain was in his early twenties. Jai Singh was therefore only a boy when he succeeded him but was destined to rule for forty eight years. His long tenure gave him ample time to develop the estate despite the many challenges he faced from diverse quarters. The arts flourished during his rule as numerous paintings found in the 'Jot Dans' testify. The long years of rule enabled him to have many of his portraits executed and to indulge in diverse pursuits and interests. There is a portrait of him as a young ruler holding a flower in his hand on a terrace in the midst of flowering groves in the style of Mughal nobility. In another, he is gorgeously attired in an exquisite gold brocade tunic riding a dark horse with attendants waving fly-whisks and a pet Cocker Spaniel running alongside. The portrait is extravagantly studded with rubies and pearls and impressed with gold leaf. Yet another shows him holding court. In later years he is shown as attired in a grey duffle coat while the horse he rides is masked and cloaked in the style of the steeds of medieval knights. As the Mughal influences recede one notes the development of interest in European fashions and pursuits. Jai Singh is a sterling example of the transition from the medieval to the dawning modern age in the eighteenth century. The magnificent costumes, leisurely pursuits and commissioning of costly portraits, indicate the growing prosperity of the fiefdom.

Yet, early in his career he faced insurmountable challenges from his own kin, the great house of Marwar. The Sanad which his father had secured from Bahadur Shah was not acknowledged by Maharaja Ajit Singh. The decline of the Mughal Empire meant that its grants were ignored with impunity when it did not suit powerful regional overlords. Maharaja Ajit Singh, the regional strongman coveted Ajmer and having failed in his designs during Bahadur Shah's reign made a fresh bid to subdue the chiefs of the area once again. In 1714 he sent a force under Sher Singh against Masuda. The Eastern gate of the fort, 'Fateh Burj' was bombarded with cannons. Jai Singh surrendered before the might of Marwar and Sher Singh

Jai Singh

was declared Hakim, the administrator of Masuda. In recent times, when the fort was being renovated by a descendant, the cannon balls were unearthed reminding him of the challenges his ancestors had faced.

Jai Singh neither knuckled under, nor forsook his patrimony. He hastened to Delhi to plead with the Padishah in the same manner as his father had done. At Delhi Bahadur Shah had been succeeded by his son Jahandar Shah who was however murdered within a year. His nephew Farukh Shiyar then succeeded to the throne. The Raja of Kishengarh in the Ajmer region who had also been divested of his kingdom by Ajit Singh approached the emperor and convinced him that the rising ambitions of the Maharaja needed to be curbed. Farukh Shiyar sent a force under the Amir-ul-Umra, the senior most noble to invade Jodhpur. He confronted Ajit Singh and pursued him from pillar to post. Ajit finally capitulated in 1714 and sought to have a rapprochement with the Mughals. According to one source he even gave his daughter in marriage to Farukh Shiyar as a mark of his sincerity and agreed to send his son Abhay to the court, promising to appear later in person whenever summoned. Incidentally this was also the last time a Rajput princess would wed a Mughal. With the decline in the power of the Mughals they were no longer considered an eligible match.

Jai Singh meanwhile had availed of the opportunity offered by the subjugation of Maharaja Ajit to press his case before the emperor. Farukh Shiyar had immediately responded favourably by issuing a Firman ordering the Parganah of Masuda to be restored to Jai Singh. After securing the Firman from Farukh Shiyar, Jai Singh was left in peace for a while.

After Farukh Shiyar's murder by the Sayyid brothers with whom Ajit Singh had developed good relations he was able to bring back his daughter, performing purification ceremonies for reconversion to Hinduism and rehabilitation within the Rajput fold.

In Rajasthan also the regional powers vied with one another to occupy Ajmer, the Mughal Suba headquarters. Maharaja Ajit Singh taking advantage of the declining Mughal control occupied Ajmer n 1720. However, before he could do any mischief in creating problems for the Ajmer Chiefs he was assassinated in his sleep in 1724 by his second son Bakhat Singh. Thus one who had no compunctions in attacking and usurping the fiefs of his kinsmen, ironically himself became a victim of patricide. His eldest son Abhay succeeded to the throne.

Then arose another threat, this time from Jaipur. In 1730, Raja Sawai Jai Singh in hot pursuit of an offending Thakur of Parsoli who had taken asylum with the Merats of Masuda, attacked the neighbouring principality of Badnore, thinking he was sheltering there. Jai Singh of Masuda saw advantage in making a strategic alliance with Badnore and Mewar forces and together they frustrated Sawai Jai Singh's attempt to invade Merwara. Jai Singh had been aware for some time of Mewar's own designs for extending its territory beyond Badnore to encompass Masuda in the North. Having assisted in repulsing Jaipur, Jai Singh of Masuda

**Jai Singh**

now moved to procure his ransom. An agreement was concluded with Mewar that its boundaries would not extend beyond the village of Saderia. South of the village would lie the boundaries of the Badnore fief and in the North Masuda. Thus acknowledgement of the boundary was secured, safeguarding for all times Masuda's territorial integrity.

Ajmer remained a bone of contention for all powers in the region. After the assassination of Maharaja Ajit Singh, Sawai Jai Singh annexed Ajmer. On his death in 1743, Maharaja Abhay Singh recaptured it in 1743 and Jodhpur once again became the premier power in the region.

While the tug of war for Ajmer had been going on in Rajasthan, major developments were taking place elsewhere in North India. The scourge of yet another Muslim invasion shook the diminishing empire to its roots. Nadir Shah having entrenched himself in Persia, Kabul and Gazni, invaded India in 1738. After the Mughal Emperor's surrender, pillage and slaughter reminiscent of the Gaznavi, Ghori and Timurian invasions ensured bleeding Delhi white. The Persian invader fortunately returned home but with an immense booty consisting of the entire Mughal treasury, including the fabled Peacock Throne. Not only had the Mughal Empire all but collapsed but even its throne had been hijacked.

In 1748 with no central power in India, the Afghan chief Ahmad Shah Abdali felt tempted to follow in the footsteps of Nadir Shah. His invasion however was repulsed at Sirhind by the combined armies of the Nawab-Vazir, Safdar-Jung and the Marathas. The empire was now in tatters. Punjab in the hands of the Afghans, Safdar-Jung the sovereign of Oudh, Aliwardi Khan supreme at Agra and Gujarat and Malwa in the hands of the Marathas.

In 1749 Maharaja Abhay Singh of Jodhpur passed away and was succeeded by Ram Singh. A dispute between him and his uncle, the patricide Bakhat Singh, resulted in a division of the loyalty of the nobility between the two sides. The Ajmer Chiefs willy nilly were obliged to take sides in this internecine conflict. Jai Singh of Masuda chose to back Ram Singh and send his son Shyam Singh to join the forces of Ram Singh's father-in-law, Raja Ishwari Singh of Jaipur and the Maratha Chief Malhar Rao Holkar. Bakhat Singh was supported by the rulers of Bikaner and Kishengarh. Bakhat Singh emerged victorious. The battle was waged near Ajmer in 1749 in which Shyam Singh of Masuda was killed. In death he was honoured as a 'Jhunjar' – a warrior who remains riding in the saddle even after being decapitated. At the family enclosure in Masuda there is a shrine to commemorate his martyrdom. Jai Singh's second son Sujan Singh was also subsequently killed in a scuffle in 1754. These regional conflicts took a heavier toll for the Ajmer chiefs than during their services to the Mughals.

In 1751 Bakhat Singh captured the fort of Jodhpur overthrowing Ram Singh. Bakhat Singh died soon thereafter and was succeeded by his son Bijay as the new Maharaja. The Marathas supporting the claims of Ram Singh invaded Jodhpur obliging Bijay Singh to cede Ajmer to them and apportioning some districts to

Ram Singh for his maintenance. In the civil war which renewed in Marwar between Bijay Singh and Ram Singh, the fiefs of Masuda and Kharwa continued to support Ram Singh whereas other fiefs of Bhinai, Dali, Tantoti supported Bijay. A pitched battle for supremacy over Ajmer took place at the village of Lamba in Masuda. The battle went in favour of Ram Singh with Maratha support and he secured some eastern districts of Marwar and Ajmer. Ram Singh eventually gave up the confrontation with Bijay and retired to settle in Jaipur in 1758. The Marathas were now in complete control of Ajmer and became the Subedars.

Some of the Ajmer chiefs offended by the Maratha chief's arrogant behaviour imprisoned him in a fortress. Jai Singh who had cultivated friendship with the Marathas as a defence against the threat from Marwar, hastened to inform Mahadji Sindhiya of these developments. Maratha reinforcements arrived and the Subedar was freed. The Marathas rewarded Jai Singh with the grant of villages of Ratakot and Muthania where Jai Singh made his subsidiary chief from Lamba as Kiledar. Jai Singh's Maratha policy had begun to pay dividends.

Jai Singh had lost two sons in battle but a third, Samrat Singh survived. The mother of this son was the princess of Samod, a fief in Jaipur. Being also his favourite Rani, she demanded that he recognize Samrat as his heir. Jai Singh however on a point of principle nominated the son of his eldest son Shyam Singh as the rightful heir. Thus the martyred Shyam Singh's son Ratan Singh became heir apparent. The Rani in a huff left for Samod with her son Samrat declaring that one day God would right this injustice. These were prophetic words, for several generations later, a descendent of Samrat Singh did indeed succeed to the throne when all other branches of the family failed in providing male issues. Samrat had been given the Jagir of Nandwara in Masuda for maintenance, from where a descendent would eventually succeed to the Gaddi.

Jai Singh after dexterously handling the numerous challenges of his rule died of natural causes at a ripe old age in 1761.

# 9

# Rise of British Power

## Ratan Singh (1761 - 1784)

When Rattan Singh succeeded to the 'Gaddi', the Marathas had just suffered a major setback at Panipat at the hands of the Afghan, Ahmad Shah, the Mughal Vazir of Oudh, and the Rohillas. The British were well entrenched in Bengal and had deposed one Nawab and replaced him with another. In 1764 the Nawab-Vazir of Oudh and the puppet Padishah suffered a crushing defeat at the hands of the British at Buxer. The Nawab-Vazir now became a vassal of the British and the Mughal Emperor a pensioner of the East India Company when Lord Clive returned to India as Governor of Bengal. The revenues of Bengal now flowed into the Company's coffers. Later in 1772 came Warren Hastings as Governor General. With the storming of the fort at Gwalior and the subjugation of Mahadji Scindhia, with whom a treaty was concluded, the British now emerged as the premier power in India. The Deccan was witnessing the rising power of Tipu Sultan at Carnatak. The other centre of power in the Deccan was the Nizam, under British influence.

Bijai Singh of Marwar was still active, though the Mahattas had denied him control over Ajmer. Defying the Maratha fiat, in 1761 he sent his agent Baboji Joshi to extract illicit revenues from the Ajmer Chiefs, while the Marathas were busy licking their wounds following their debacle at Panipat. The agent hastily recovered 20,000 dinars each from Masuda, Kharwa and Pisangan, 22,000 from Bhinai and 17,000 thousand from Govindgarh. Over 100,000 dinars were thus collected. Mahadji Scindhia's forces meanwhile arrived at Sambhar and gave chase to Baboji who lifting the siege of Ajmer, fled. Mahadji built a number of garrison fortresses on his way to Ajmer which are still standing at several places in Masuda itself. Mahadji also stayed at Masuda in view of the friendly relations the Mahattas enjoyed with the Masuda Chiefs.

The constant threats from the neighbourhood are highlighted by an incident in 1777, showing that Mewar's desire to usurp the Masuda Parganah of Jagmalot

Ratan Singh

Mertia's, just north of its Jaimalot Mertia fiefdom of Badnore, remained undiminished despite the boundary agreement in the time of Jai Singh. Thus a hundred Mewaris from the village Khari-ka-Lamba were encouraged to encroach on the fertile Jalia area of Masuda north of the river Khari and began to plough the land. A force was despatched from Masuda with Kanwar Gaj Singh and Kothari Jai Karan and a skirmish ensued at village Baral where the Kothari was wounded by a gun-shot. Three persons from Masuda and four from Khari-ka-Lamba lost their lives but the intruders were beaten back. A Mewar force under Nathu Shah, Chunda and Anopji Agarwal then arrived and camped across the river, leaving little doubt that the incident had been instigated at the behest of the Maharana. Ratan Singh now saw fit to face this affront and led a force, camping at Jalia north of the river. The Mewar force then raided and looted Jalia establishing a Thana there. The Hakim of the area sought to settle the dispute, it being finally decided that the Khari River would henceforth form the boundary. Village Girnar belonging to Masuda was ceded to Mewar, though the temple of the goddess Girnar Rai remained with Masuda. Thus another threat from Mewar was contained.

Merwara also remained an area coveted by all the provincial powers, posing a continuous threat to the fiefdom of Masuda. In 1778 an army was sent from Jodhpur to capture Chang and Kot Kirama in Merwara. Ratan Singh realized that if Merwara came under Marwar's hegemony, Masuda would lose this important buffer and be under perpetual threat. This was particularly so because his predecessors had given support to Bijay Singh's rival Ram Singh and the former wanted to teach the Masuda Chiefs a lesson. He therefore pooled all his resources to support the Merwara chiefs against the attempted takeover. Masuda and the Merwara chiefs succeeded in repulsing the Marwar campaign.

These incidents amply illustrate the constant threat which the big powers of the region posed for the little feudatories and it is a tribute to their determination, valour, courage and ability that they managed to defend their territory against severe odds to survive into the twentieth century with the area they had conquered more or less in tact.

Threats from regional powers were not the only ones which the chiefs encountered. Another incident illustrates how even normal daily life was full of unexpected perils. No one could really be trusted. Court intrigue and jealousies, the ambitions of brothers and even sons could quickly translate into treachery, poisoned bandages, lethal potions, a push from a balcony or being assassinated while asleep. For Ratan Singh it came in the shape of a Sadhu. Received and welcomed into his private chambers in the Masuda Fort this Amar Singh suddenly assaulted him with intent to kill. His attendants Naharji Tak, Fatta Hazuri and Bhupat Gaur rushed to his defence. The last two were killed but Amar Singh was wounded and arrested. The records do not reveal the reasons for his murderous assault. The survivor Tak was awarded a large area of land in gratitude. Today it still goes by the name of Takon-ka-Beer which is appropriately a demonstration farm under the Panchayat Samiti Masuda.

Ratan Singh

Ratan Singh during his rule engaged in several important development activities in his estate. Ratan Sagar Bandh built during his time proved to be the first important irrigation project and benefits cultivators to this day. He also built several small water reservoirs called Nadis to encourage agriculture. In 'Pattas' authorizing land to cultivators he urged them to increase cultivation, manifold with the words "Ouche Jito Bauje", cultivate intensively. Beers or grass reservoirs and shrub forests were developed with 'Begars', grass depots as reserves to meet shortages in times of famine. Stocks of grain were also built to meet the requirements during drought.

In defence of the Parganah he sought to ensure a cavalry of 800 horses to be available at all times through contributions by the 'Jamayat' of Thikanedars, Jagirdars and Bhumias. Jagirs for increasing cultivated areas were farmed out to Rajputs from other clans including the Taks, Bagads, Parihars, Sinthals, Sankhalas, Kachawa, Mertias, Tanwars, Chundawats etc. These Jagirs were in addition to those of the Mertia Jagmalot brethren. Fresh hamlets or 'Dhanis' were created where Jats and Gujar farmers displaced from unstable regions of Rajputana and elsewhere through wars or on account of the atrocities of landlords, were encouraged to settle in Masuda. Being a small fief, there was greater security for them with easier access to the Chief for redressing grievances.

Ratan Singh did not neglect to have himself portrayed in miniature paintings. The 'Jot-Dans' have at least two surviving portraits which give an idea about his life and times. One is on horseback, splendidly attired in saffron flowing robes and contrasting red headdress elongated like a bee-hive with tassels and plumes without a trace of the Mughal influence. The attendant leading the cortège with a mace surprisingly has a Maratha Headwear, doubtless a legacy of Mahadji Sindhia's visits to the fort. Another holds a hubble-bubble whose pipe and spout Ratan Singh deliberately holds in his hand close to his mouth, in the process of pulling in a puff of aromatic smoke laced with opium. The other attendant with a fly-whisk has a similar convoluted bee-hive headgear. The trace of hair on his chin defines him as a young Muslim confidant. Ratan's 'Angarkha' tunic is no longer Mughal knee length but reaches down in pleated folds to his ankles. The fashions in dress have changed with the decline of the empire. The horse is an Arab, but now stylized and robust, having lost all the realism of the Mughal brush. The nether regions of the horse are orange with henna, entirely Rajput in inspiration. But this can still be classified as a miniature of the Ajmer school. It has superb quality and finesse though totally devoid of Mughal influence and marching forward into a world of Marathas with the encroaching influence of Marwar, yet maintaining the unique character of the Ajmer school – Poetry in motion in the paint.

The other portrait shows him seated on his cushions, the 'Gadi-Mora', receiving another Ajmer chief who appears to have taken the needless precaution of bringing his decorous shield with him. Again Ratan is seen with his addictive hubble-bubble, the spout raised close to his lips and surprisingly the same Muslim attendant who earlier wielded a fly-whisk, this time holding a staff with the same bee-hive headdress. This attendant was unquestionably a favourite confidant.

It will be recalled that Ratan Singh's uncle Samrat Singh had left for Samod in Jaipur with his mother when she expressed grave reservations about his succession to the Gaddi in preference to her son. It appears however that Ratan visited Jaipur often to be with his uncle to see the splendours of the Amber Fort and the remarkable city which Jai Singh built, the Hawa Mahal and the wonders of the Jantar Mantar astrological observatory. This inspired him to create within Masuda Fort a Chand Mahal, a Kach Mahal, a Badal Mahal and a Suraj Mahal. These Mahals were decorated with murals depicting the ancestors and their stately processions. In the Kach Mahal he sought to replicate the excellent work of the Amber palace where a candle light would be magnified a thousand fold in the reflected light of mirror mosaics on the walls. In the Chander Mahal he sought to replicate the astrological splendours of the planetary systems, the 'Grahas', on the ceiling. Frescos of Krishna Lila were also depicted on the walls and there was a mural showing the Hawa Mahal in the background with Ratan Singh seated before it.

Unfortunately these amazing art frescos were demolished by a descendant, Bijay Singh in the 1920s in a fit of modernization when he sought to renovate the fort and build modern apartments in their place. It was only when the art master at Mayo College, B.C. Gue, expressed a keenness to see the planetary systems in the Chander Mahal that he had learnt about at Shantiniketan's School of Art, that he was informed that tragically they were no longer in existence. However some traces of the defaced murals can still be seen in some corners of the fort.

It is evident that Ratan Singh was a chief not only concerned with survival and the defence of his fiefdom but was also deeply concerned with preserving and promoting the arts inspired by what he witnessed at the palaces at Jaipur which he sought in his humble way to replicate in distant Masuda.

Ratan Singh died in 1784 leaving three sons, Bhairon Singh the eldest, Bhopal Singh and Dev Singh.

# 10

# The Maratha Factor

## Bhairon Singh (1784 - 1806)

It was during the rule of Bhairon Singh that the British emerged as the paramount power in India. Most powers submitted to British suzerainty one by one in return for security and protection. The Nawab of Oudh became a vassal and the Mughal Emperor a puppet pensioner of the company. The Nizam, the Peshwa and Gaikwar were treaty bound not to wage wars or enter into treaty without the consent of the Governor General, Sindhia had lost influence over Delhi and territory north of the Jamuna. The rising power of Tipu Sultan in the Carnatak was the last to be curbed and finally extinguished with his defeat and death at Saringapatam. Yet the British did not extend their 'protection' to the Rajputs. Scindhia and Holkar were left free to plunder Rajputana, resulting in anarchy. The advent of the British into Rajputana would take place during the life of Bhairon Singh's successor.

The Ajmer chiefs soon realized that the Maratha was no friend or well wisher. His sole interest was to extract revenue through imposition of Chauth and Sardeshmukhi. The garrison fortresses built by Mahadji Sindhia were not symbols of defence as the other forts of Rajasthan, but centres of exploitation. The garrison fortresses enabled the Marathas to interfere in day to day affairs of the fiefdom while indulging in looting excursions at will. Mewar was already reeling under the incessant demands of the Marathas and its coffers were empty.

The time had come for Bhairon Singh to distance himself from the Marathas and ally with Marwar. What precipitated matters were the unending raids of the Maratha gangs. Constant vigil had to be maintained by placing drums at high points on hills to warn of approaching Maratha raiders and shutting the gates of the town when warned. What would follow was a siege or a skirmish. The drummers on the hills came to be known as 'Sena'. There is a hill near Masuda village which still goes by the name of Seni-Magra. The drums were gigantic and one surviving into the twentieth century was used in the marriage of a daughter of a descendant to the Kanwar of Mandawa in the 1940s, to store water sufficient for the entire marriage party. Those Thakurs and Zamindars who didn't concede to the Maratha demands were summarily ousted without any consultation with the Chief of the fief. Thus one Thikanedar, Sathana was deposed and another, Ramgarh, a favourable agreement was concluded in return for his cooperation in building a Maratha fortress in his area. These arbitrary actions undermined the authority of the Chief. The Marathas had scant regard for the position or sensitivities of the Chief.

An appeal for redressal to a higher authority as on the days of Mughal power, was no longer available. Bhairon Singh had to suffer the humiliation in silence, biding his time. The chiefs of the neighbouring fiefdom of Kharwa, Surajmal, suffering the same fate had confided in Bhairon Singh that in his father's time Maharaja Bijai Singh of Marwar during a visit to Pushkar near Ajmer for pilgrimage had in talks proposed some plan for the ouster of the Deccan menace, as the Marathas were called. He proposed that it was time to seek the support of Marwar, the lesser of the two evils.

The opportunity finally arrived when the Marathas, now more strident than ever in extracting revenues from Rajputana, attacked Jaipur. Jodhpur sent an army under Singhvi Dhanraj to help Jaipur. Bhairon Singh joined with a force of his own, against what had now emerged as a common enemy. The small Masuda detachment was led by his brother Bhopal Singh. In the face of this concerted Rajput defence, the Maratha attack led by the French artillery commander 'De-Boigne's two battalions was reversed at the battle of Tunga.

Mr. Compton a European chronicler who witnessed the battle is quoted in the book by the eminent historian of Rajput affairs. Harbilas Sharda : "The Rathores of Jodhpur, the very flower of Rajput bravery .... as they came within sight of De-Boigne's two battalions .... rent the air with fierce and exalting shouts .... their flags fluttering in the breeze, the sun glinted on their plumed helmets and chain armour and their swords and spears flashed aloft as they thundered over the sun-baked plane. It was a terrible baptism of battle for De-Boigne's young battalions."

The records state that Chundawat Sangram Singh, Deva Dhabhai and Harnath Singh Charan with twenty two others from Masuda were killed in battle. The above reveals that the force of horsemen was constituted of diverse castes and groups all being honourably mentioned in the records without discrimination.

When Bhopal Singh returned from Tunga, in appreciation, Bhairon Singh arranged for him to succeed to the large Thikana of Shergarh where there had been no issue. With growing proximity towards Marwar and hope of securing their protection against the Maratha menace, a tacit acknowledgement of their overlord status followed by the acceptance of a Sanad from Jodhpur and the consequent return of the Thikana of Sathana back to its rightful Thakur from the Jagmalot 'Bhayat', in defiance of the Marathas.

Suffering a reverse in 1787 at Tunga, Mahadji Sindhia struck at Patan securing a victory over Jaipur. He then marched towards Ajmer to avenge the defeat in 1790. His forces were again led by De-Boigne. The defence of Ajmer was entrusted by Jodhpur to the Ajmer fiefdoms. Bhopal Singh of Masuda, Surajmal of Kharwa, the Raja of Bhinai, Bakht Singh of Deolia and Gulab Singh of Tantoti joined forces led by Jodhpur's Singhvi Dhanraj. De-Boigne placed his guns on the hills around the lake Ana Sagar and bombarded the town. The city walls collapsed and ten thousand Maratha horsemen charged into town. The gates were treacherously opened by some Muslim elements and the Marathas commenced to loot and plunder the city. The Taragarh fort remained under siege. Suddenly and inexplicably Maharaja Bijai Singh, appearing to lose resolve wrote to the Kharwa Chief to hand over the fort to the 'Deccanis'. Dhanraj unable to accept this humiliating surrender after their staunch defence, committed suicide by swallowing crushed diamond powder. Ajmer fell back into the hands of the Marathas. Their preoccupations in the Doab, however resulted in the grip on Ajmer being at best tenuous. Marwar continued to plot and plan to displace them.

In 1801 at Pushkar an important nuptial was underway. Bijai Singh's grandson and heir Bhim Singh was being married to the sister of Maharaja Pratap Singh of Jaipur, while the latter was to wed Bhim Singh's sister. The Ajmer chiefs happily joined in to celebrate the dual alliance being consecrated in their quarter. Bhairon Singh for the first time also joined in a Marwar marriage ceremony.

For the Ajmer chiefs survival thus meant a discreet dual strategy of maintaining cordiality with both parties. Bhairon Singh was careful not to adopt an adversarial position with the Marathas. In 1791 Scindhia had placed Shivaji Nana in charge of Ajmer. The chief of Bhinai, Raja Udai Bhan, unable to tolerate interference had resorted to capturing and imprisoning Rao Bhao a Maratha officer. Shivaji Nana's son Vishwapat then attacked Bhinai and got Rao Bhao released. The Bhinai Raja was imprisoned at Ajmer. Bhairon Singh took no action to support the Raja, thereby earning the favour of the Marathas again. This paid dividends later as we shall see during the rule of his successor.

Bhairon Singh while maintaining cordial relations with the Marathas, did not neglect to extend due courtesies to Marwar either. Thus Bhairon Singh succeeded in walking the right rope between Jodhpur and the Marathas with tact and discretion safeguarding the interests of his estate and dynasty.

Bhairon Singh followed his father's example in devoting attention to irrigation projects. The Bhaironsagar Bandh was built and a village developed next to it called Bhaironkhera after his name. Despite his initiatives to develop irrigation projects and develop agriculture in his fiefdom, the arts appear to have been neglected. The absence of any paintings of the period or any portraiture of Bhairon Singh indicates that the turbulent times left no opportunity to indulge in fine arts. The fall of the Mughal Empire and unsettled conditions arising from the depredations of the Marathas and the regional tug of war for Ajmer had devastated the economy. Security was affected to such an extent that the only priority left was survival. It is therefore not surprising that we do not fiend a single portrait of

Bhairon Singh, making him an exception in the collection of ancestral portraits. Fortunately his successor Devi Singh revived the passion for the arts with abundant portraiture, painting and commitment to the fine arts. Bhairon Singh died in 1806 leaving two sons, Devi Singh and Padam Singh.

In closing this chapter we need to analyse the phenomena of the Maratha sojourn in Rajpurtana. The genius of the Marathas in acquiring a domineering position in India cannot but be admired. Their cohesive and purposeful mastery of the four quarters of the subcontinent from pockets in Konkan, overcoming the regional Adil Shahi power, to wielding power in imperial Delhi, Bengal, Punjab and Rajputana and bid for empire are only paralleled by the Mughal and the British. That they failed in achieving this honourable goal of Hindu Pad Padshahi, establishing an indigenous empire by throwing off an alien yoke, could be explained as a tragic accident of history.

# 11

# Company Rule at Ajmer

## Devi Singh (1806 – 1843)

Devi Singh was a veritable Hercules in form and strength. If we are to believe the Khayats he could twist out a Chittori coin between his thumb and forefinger, tear a rhinoceros shield in two with his bare hands, raise a camel an inch above the ground, placing his hands under its chest 'thumbi' and crack open dried coconuts in his armpits ! Likewise he consumed over a quarter 'seer' of 'Kalakand' milk cakes for breakfast. His portraits show a Spartan, robust warrior dressed in a plain white cotton ankle length Angarkha tunic with a simple red sash hanging from his shoulder. His habit was devoid of any sequence, embroidery or printed design. He is shown armed with a spear and sword, a shield strapped to his back, ready for battle. His attendants striding briskly next to his horse hold royal insignia but no leisurely fly-whisk, with shields strapped to their backs, rustic village style turbans loosely wound round the head. Devi Singh's head gear is decidedly Maratha with a gold band.

He has a fine dark beard kept firmly in place, hugging the contours of his jaw. The artist has painted a superb Arab horse, friskily rearing on its hind legs. The proportions of the horse are rotund with the full effect of poetic license which is the stamp of Marwar paintings. Man and animal are derived from fixed prototypical images in the artist's mind barely recognizable as the person being portrayed. These are poetical definitions and stereotypes of Chief, attendant and horse and distant abstract puffs of cloud on the horizon. The formality, precision, realism and hairline detail of the exquisite Mughal miniatures have been replaced by the Jodhpur School's passionate and robust geometrical rhythms. The blocks of colours provide contrast and perspective and a pronounced sense of deliberate informality bordering on caricature when the last attendant has one leg still left out of the frame of the painting while the one leading the horse has already begun to step right out of the frame, giving the impression that the group has attained such galloping motion that it can no longer be restrained by the frame.

**Devi Singh**

The adoption of the style of the Jodhpur School of miniatures and the Maratha headgear tells their own tale of the new influences marking the epoch. All other portraits of Devi Singh are also painted in the Marwar style of painting. They portray an athletic hunter bending over a horse to plunge his lance into a tiger on a hunt. Another is a grand wide angle canvas showing him holding court with dancing girls performing the 'Ghumar' pirouettes, their skirts filling in the process, with musicians in accompaniment. There are numerous paintings of women with stylized eyes shaped like fish (Meenakshi) playing the yo-yo or holding peacocks or dancing holding hands. While the faces are all stereotype, they are not clones and an attempt has been made to provide distinctive features, headgears and beards. Yet all portraits of the Marwar School are far removed from realism and allow poetic exaggeration. The effect is nevertheless startling and aesthetically pleasing, making the Marwar style no less artistic than the paintings of the Ajmer School were, one may say even as Picasso's abstractions are masterpieces to match the works of the Classical Age.

It is evident that with the arrival of the British and the imposition of a more settled order and administration, the Masuda Chief had been enabled to nurse his passion for reviving the arts in painting, dance, music and games of leisure.

By 1806 the British had emerged as the paramount power. However, Lord Wellesley the Governor General's brilliant successes had unnerved the British Parliament which wanted the benefits of trade while observing a policy of non-intervention. In view of slow communications however, Wellesley's policies had resulted in the fait accompli of British suzerainty. For a time a rule was followed of no interference whatsoever in the internal affairs of the principalities unless absolutely necessary. This interference took place when the principality was threatened with ruin. The British found that generally in the Rajput states the treasuries were empty, revenue mortgaged to bankers and money lenders for years. No further loans were forthcoming except with British guarantees. Meanwhile money was always required to pay the mercenary and standing armies. British agents sent to the court for maintaining relations were entreated by the rulers to help in securing loans. British urgings for gradual disbursement of mercenaries and reduction in expenditure were met with opposition from the courtiers and nobility who had vested interests in continuing as before. British sanction was also now required for legitimizing succession and appointment of Regents during the minority of rulers. British intervention was necessitated when rival clans clashed on issues of succession or in protecting rulers against plots to overthrow them. From 1818-25 the British were forced to intervene to restore order in the states of Jaipur, Bharatpur and Gwalior.

Rajput principalities had submitted to British suzerainty in return for protection from the Marathas. Holkar's sorties into Rajasthan and his attempt to act as the emperor's proxy at Delhi had also been challenged. Yet for more than a decade after Devi Singh ascended the Gaddi of Masuda, the full force of British suzerainty was not felt in the Ajmer region and for the Ajmer Chiefs life continued as before.

Devi Singh's rule proved to be a long and momentous one of over three decades. Before the arrival of the British in Ajmer in 1818 the Marathas continued to be active in the region. Daulat Rao Sindhia was in the process of plundering Mewar and had encamped at Badnore to the south of the Khari river in 1809. In 1812 Kanwar Jodh Singh of Badnore sought help against his father. Devi readily obliged against his Mewar foe the Badnore Thakur. The town of Tunkarwar was seized and handed over to Jodh Singh. In the ensuing battle with the Thakur of Badnore a Masuda force was joined by Maratha reinforcement from Ajmer. Thakur Jait Singh was defeated, Badnore artillery captured and the Marathas were paid for their help. No support had come for Badnore from Mewar which was already in dire straits on accounts of Maratha depredations. The boundary was redrawn with agreements signed between Jodh Singh and Devi Singh, witnessed by Thakur Bhairon Singh of Baghsuri. The Marathas decided the boundary dispute between Badnore and Masuda in the latter's favour on account of traditionally cordial relations with Masuda. Local chiefs deciding boundary agreements without the sanctions of the regional overlords heretofore had been unheard of, but it was a sign of the decline of Mewar's power.

Devi Singh during his rule remained aggressive and strident in his dealings with the Thakurs of his fief. The Thakur of Ramgarh in Masuda had for some time been playing a dubious role with Maratha support ever since he had permitted them to build a fortress at his village. While Devi Singh was passing by Ramgarh, shots were fired from a hill in an attempt to assassinate him. Devi then marched with a force of five hundred horse and ransacked Ramgarh. Thakur Parasramji was captured and Ramgarh confiscated. When another Thakur, of Kirap, died issue less and his adoptive successor was unable to pay the 'Jama' dues, the Thikana was annexed.

Devi Singh also moved against the Thikana of Sathana within Masuda for non payment of dues. In the skirmish an attendant of the Thakur was killed. He was the only son of an old mother who in grief and rage pronounced a curse on the Masuda chiefs, that having lost her only issue, for three generations the Masuda Chiefs would suffer the same fate. In India both blessings and curses, especially from the aggrieved if weak and defenceless, are taken seriously as often they prove to be oracular pronouncements. Indeed for three generations from Devi Singh there were no male issues to succeed to the Gaddi.

Devi Singh also laboured to cultivate social relations with the big power of Jodhpur, Jaipur and Mewar and the tribal chiefs of neighbouring Merwara. In 1813 he went to Roopnagar to attend the marriage of Man Singh of Jodhpur and Jagat Singh of Jaipur, with an entourage of 150 horse, 22 camels and 30 attendants according to the Khayats. He regularly invited the Mer chiefs of Jhak, Lulwa and Shyamgarh at Dussera and other festivals to be entertained at Masuda. They would be received at the Marwari Darwaza, the western town gate, with drums and insignia (Nagara and Nishan) and in the Durbar were offered Tazim honours in the shape of 'Amal-Galma', opium water, in the highest expression of friendship.

The greatest of the Mer chiefs, the Khan of Athoon was also a frequent visitor. Thereafter the Mers would indulge in plundering regions of Marwar and Mewar. Devi Singh did not hesitate to provide a support of a force of 500 horse to back them on these expeditions. This contingent was specially maintained for assisting the Mers. In return they paid him Chauth. To this day the tribal Mers and Merats of Masuda area are called 'Chauth-Batees'.

Devi Singh also attended a Durbar of the Udaipur Maharana. This is not surprising considering that Masuda was located on the northern border of Mewar. Hearing about his phenomenal strength, the Maharana asked him to tear apart a Rhino Shield. He tore half of it and asked the Maharana to have one of his august nobility, the Umraos, to complete the job, but none were equal to the task. The myths and epics are often inspiration for such acts of bravado and one is reminded of Lord Rama succeeding in breaking the bow of Shiva at the court of Janak to win the hand of Sita, after all other notable kings had failed to do so. Pleased with Devi Singh's feat the Maharana wanted to gift him a Parganah. Detecting an ulterior motive he declined the generous offer saying he preferred to rule a small principality rather than be a grander Jagirdar of Mewar. This spirit of fierce independence was not uncommon among Ajmer chiefs who for centuries had defended their independent status against great odds. Any servility, however partial, to regional overlords would have meant a sudden change in status and freedom.

However, all these local events paled into insignificance in the floodlights of the arrival of the British in 1818 at the erstwhile Mughal Suba headquarters of Ajmer. The Ajmer chiefs would have watched from the corner of their eyes as the 'Firangis' of Sir Thomas Roe's ilk suddenly burst upon their world with Sir David Ochterlony's (now General) cavalry's hoofs resounding in the vicinity. He arrived imperiously to take over the city from the Maratha Subedar Bapu Sindhia and despatched his emissaries forthwith to the Ajmer fiefdoms to inform them of the historic change in command. Unfortunately the Ajmer chiefs failed to grasp the gravity of the moment, treating it as yet another passing phenomenon in the fortunes of their Suba headquarters. Ajmer had changed hands so often after the Mughals that they cannot be entirely faulted for their myopic inability to appreciate the momentous developments. The Padishah was after all still known to be in Delhi at the Red Fort and the honourable East India Company under whose authority Ochterlony was acting was so ambiguous a concept that it quite escaped their comprehension. Unable to take the developments seriously, they failed in extending any courtesy either to the emissary or to present themselves at Ajmer before General Ochterlony. They did not deem it necessary to enter into treaties for legitimizing their positions with the new masters.

Livid at this arrogant and callous attitude of the Ajmer chiefs, Ochterlony demanded from Wilder, the new superintendent of Ajmer an immediate assessment of the status and legitimacy of the erring chiefs. Wilder was also the officer in charge of such mighty vassals such as Jodhpur, Jaisalmer and Kishangarh.

Col. Wilder besieges Masuda–Company Panting mid 19th Century

Wilder dismissed them as opium-eating, slovenly lords, highly indebted and completely under the influence of their 'Kamdars', the chief revenue administrators.

This was of course a hasty and inaccurate first impression. The chiefs, though unfamiliar with the Anglo-Saxon etiquette were far from being incompetent, slovenly lords, considering their amazing skills at surviving diverse and significant threats from all and sundry for centuries. Offering and consuming opium were essential eastern etiquette and necessary tranquillizers in a situation of continuous warfare. It need not have meant consumption of opium in excess of such requirements or necessarily an addiction.

The issue was debated back and forth and at one point Col. Wilder had even suggested outright annexation or confiscation of the smaller fiefs around Ajmer. The correspondence continued after Ochterlony's return to Delhi. Wilder claimed he found no Sanads with many of the chiefs or any reliable document to establish their legitimacy. Ochterlony and Wilder came to the conclusion that the chiefs could summarily be swept aside and duly compensated as a mark of British justice and magnanimity. However, saner counsel prevailed. Consecutive officers like Middleton and Cavendish found that the chiefs had received recognition from successive governments and authorities of the area and Sanads may have got lost in the turbulence of the times. They also cautioned that arbitrary and precipitate elimination of the fiefs would produce a general Rajput revolt. A more prudent course would be to acknowledge their legitimacy and fix permanent tributes on the basis of incomes.

The Ajmer Istimarari (hereditary) estates had in fact never paid revenues till the time the Marathas arrived. In Mughal times the chiefs had received recognition for services to the empire by being awarded Mansabs requiring maintenance of standing forces to be put in the service of the Empire when required. They had never been required to pay land revenue.

Issues were finally settled later by the time of the visit of the Governor General Lord William Bentinck in April 1832, accepting the status and legitimacy of the Ajmer chiefs and according them an order of protocol for seating at formal functions and state processions.

General Ochterlony during his visit carried a Mughal title, Nasir-ud-daulah. The first British army cantonment established near Masuda was therefore dubbed Nasirabad. It is today a flourishing little well planned town which is home to an Indian army cantonment. Till recently it had a large population of Anglo-Indians and Parsis who felt comfortable in settling in an orderly cantonment township.

At this time the Marquise of Hastings was Governor General. He was a great disciplinarian and wanted to rid India of organized banditry and tribal lawlessness. He launched a crusade against the menace of the Pindaris who were organized gangs of dacoits, originally camp followers of the Marathas. In 1817 the British armies of Madras and Bengal finally succeeded in eliminating and disbanding this menace. Ochterlony, pursuing the Governor General's dictat was equally keen to contain the threat that the Mers posed through their banditry from their bases in Merwara adjoining areas in Marwar, Mewar and Masuda, by disturbing the peace in the region. The Ajmer superintendent Wilder was given the task to end this menace also.

Wilder was aware of Devi Singh's cultivation of the Mers and his maintenance of a force of 500 horse and equal member of footmen armed with matchlocks, guns and swords to assist the Mers. Wilder immediately proceeded with a battalion and laid siege on Masuda town. Devi Singh finally realized the gravity of the situation, faced by the invincible Firangi conquerors of Hindustan. In a complete about face he sent a message of peace, friendship and total cooperation to Wilder. The siege was lifted and he received the Sahib Wilder at a spot marked by a well called 'Mana Po', which became an important landmark. Wilder was ushered into town and the fort with ceremony, both Devi Singh and Wilder riding on stately elephants. The siege and subsequent friendly elephant ride are portrayed in Company School paintings available to this day. The Colonel then challenged the Thakur to prove his credentials. If he was indeed a friend of the British he must assist them in suppressing the Mers of his area.

Devi Singh did not hesitate to comply and with a force of 150 horse followed the Colonel into Mer territory. They jointly paraded the Mer towns of Masuda, Shyamgarh, Lulwa and Jhak in a show of force. The headmen were summoned and commanded to stop their banditry. Thanas, police posts of the British and Masuda were established in the area. But the banditry continued and the Thanas were ransacked. The rest of Merwara in adjoining areas of Marwar and Mewar also rose in rebellion. The Governor General, the Marquise of Hastings then commissioned a great force under Col. Hill to bring the Mers into submission. Infantry and cavalry at Nasirabad were joined by Devi Singh's horsemen in 1819, in a final campaign to subdue the tribes. The Mer towns were bombarded and they were finally brought to heel. In 1821 another battalion was sent to subdue the Mers of other regions. After much fighting and bloodshed in 1823 the Mers were overpowered and Tehsils were established at Todgarh, Beawar and other places. Col. Hill was appointed Assistant Superintendent of Merwara.

The areas with Mer populations were leased from Marwar, Mewar and Masuda and brought under direct British control as one unit of administration. Lease money was promised in lieu thereof. The lease was in fact a euphemism for annexation. Masuda lost vast tracts of territory including the land on which the new town Nayanagar, later to be renamed Beawar, was built as a hub for trading cotton and settling the Merwara area. The 'lease' of Masuda territory was in fact a punitive measure against Devi Singh for having been an ally and conspirator of the Mers and an accomplice in their depredations in the region.

Hill's successor Col. J. Dixon was so enamoured of the Mers that he took a Mer wife. Their son was eventually sent to England and lived and died there. Col. Dixon also founded a new town in the area called 'Nayanagar' which later came to be called Beawar, now one of the largest Mandis for cotton in Asia. Dixon identified himself totally with the proud Mer tribals, spoke their language, observed their customs and took great pains to develop Merwara. In appreciation, the British promoted him to Superintendent of the whole of Ajmer and Merwara. He died in 1853. His 'Chatri' or commemorative pavilion was built in the main square of Beawar city but after Independence, in a fit of chauvinistic fanaticism, it was destroyed.

The fiercely independent spirit of the Mer tribes thus not only won over the chiefs of Masuda but the very representative of the British Empire who was sent to subjugate and rule them succumbed to their rustic charms and indomitable spirit.

As Rajputana settled down under the new British dispensation, the Governor General thought fit to make his first visit to the region. In 1832 Lord William Bentinck visited Ajmer. The entourage accompanying him was not unlike that of the Mughal emperors of yesteryear. Elephants, camels, horses and palanquins carried the officials and their train with bullock carts bringing the luggage at the rear. The entourage travelled no more than twelve miles a day, taking three months to cover the distance from Agra and back. A cavalry of Skinners Horse accompanied him with the legendary Lt. Col. James Skinner providing an eye witness report.

The Governor General had invited all the princes of Rajputana to meet him at Ajmer. Those who complied included Maharaja Kalyan Singh of Kishengarh, Nawab Amir Khan of Tonk, Maharao Ram Singh of Kota, Maharana Jawan Singh of Udaipur, Maharaja Sawai Singh of Jaipur and Maharao Ram Singh of Bundi. Jodhpur, Jaisalmer and Bikaner sent excuses for their absence. The G.G. (Governor General) was accompanied by upwards of 100,000 cavalry and infantry and 200 pieces of cannon. The chiefs of Ajmer came in carriages with caparisoned horses to the Ana Sagar lake Bundh (Dam) and were duly instructed in the order of protocol they would henceforth enjoy. Devi Singh was in one of them viewing the new order of Firangis marching his world into the modern era.

The new order of protocol and courtesies, the uniforms of the Sepoys, the orderly and highly disciplined marches, the novel sound of trumpets, bugles, bagpipers and drummers, the British attire, headgear, gloves, boots, spats and weapons, their postures, gestures, habits and mannerisms, preferences and dislikes, cuisine and wines, would all have been carefully and eagerly noted at first hand by Davi Singh even as had been done in an earlier epoch at the Mughal Durbars at Akbar's palace near the tomb of the Khwaja. Close interaction with Col. Wilder had already conveyed to Devi Singh a sense of the British personality and way of doing things. Now in a grand magnification of this on an imperial scale the event provided a unique opportunity to watch and learn about the style and eccentricities of the new masters.

The Mughals, Mewar, Marwar and Marathas had all contributed to the style and way of life of the little courts and the influence had percolated down to the different levels of administrations and public life. Now the alien culture would also leave its indelible brand on the culture and psychology of the fiefdoms. Devi

Singh would return from the grand ceremonies, awed and impressed with the Firangis and in no doubt about their extraordinary capabilities, bringing with him many impressions and influences to imbibe. The court, the corridors of the fortress and the by lanes of the town would be abuzz with talk and animated discussions about the great event that had just transpired in neighbouring Ajmer and the new British phenomenon.

A battalion was placed at the Taragarh Fort on the hill overhanging the city to make British power abundantly visible. Gun salutes from the fort thundered across the assembly of princes and chiefs. There was no doubt left in Rajputana that the British were the new masters of Hindustan.

# 12

# Company to Crown

## Sheonath Singh (1843 - 1863)

According to popular belief, Sheonath Singh's succession was the direct consequence of the curse placed upon the House of Masuda by the bereaved old lady of Sathana. Devi Singh died without issue in 1843. Sheonath Singh would do the same and his successor Bahadur Singh would lose a son prematurely, necessitating adoption a third time in three generations, fulfilling the damning prophesy. This was in contrast to the abundant progeny of earlier generations of Rathores and the first break in natural succession since Bhupati's conquest of Masuda in 1563. Sheonath Singh was Devi Singh's brother Padam Singh's son. He was a lad of sixteen when he succeeded to the Gaddi.

The British were now firmly established at Ajmer, overlord and arbiter of all affairs in Rajputana. The Modern era had begun and Ajmer for Rajputana became the window to the outside world and a show-case of development. Soon after the arrival of Lord Dalhousie as Governor General in 1848, the Punjab and Burma were annexed and Afghans brought firmly under British control. Next followed the annexations of Oudh and Nagpur.

It was also during Lord Dalhousie's administrates that railway lines were laid down and telegraph wires hung across the length and breadth of India. Calcutta was now illuminated with gas and education was sought to be introduced throughout India. The people of the area however, steeped in orthodoxy and superstition viewed these developments with great suspicion apprehension and resentment, believing that the British were binding the land in fetters. They condemned the technology as a form of magic and sorcery. The man in the street believed that the East India Company was a demonic entity on an island in the middle of the ocean, wherefrom it sent out its enchanted ships to conquer lands.

The elite while not so gullible nevertheless regarded the British as polluted beef-eating aliens, no better than 'untouchables'. Thus Sheonath Singh, according to the Khayats, after once shaking hands with an English Officer, albeit with all

Sheonath Singh

due decorum and courtesy, refrained from touching anything until the floors had been thoroughly cleansed by the water of the holy Ganges, 'Ganga Jal', and he himself had undergone purification baths followed by a performance of 'Pujas'. Then only did he take "a draught of water and a morsel of bread in his mouth". One is not surprised at his astonishing behaviour, for a nobler and more sophisticated Maharaja Madho Singh of Jaipur even decades later carried 'Ganga Jal' in giant silver urns on his visit to London for the coronation. This was the only water he would drink during the trip overseas. His eminent ancestor Raja Man Singh three centuries earlier appears to have been less inflexible in being persuaded by Emperor Akbar through an apt couplet to overcome his inhibitions regarding defilement in crossing the boundaries across Hindustan into Afghanistan leading the Mughal armies as its commander-in-chief. Yet again even in more recent times the idea of the young Gandhi crossing the seas for education in the U.K. caused grave anguish for the family, firm in the belief that such a passage would result in defilement, loss of caste status and even entail excommunication.

It was not till much later, with the introduction of liberal education for the elite and the setting up of institutions like the Mayo College Ajmer, Rajkumar College Rajkot and Aitchison College Lahore that the British succeeded in eradicating such superstition and prejudices existing even at the highest levels of society.

Lord Dalhousie's 'Doctrine of Lapse' brought the brewing distrust and discontent to a boiling universal frenzy. The introduction of the Enfield rifle with new cartridge requiring greasing with fat of beef and pork, which had to be bitten into before loading, abhorrent both to Hindus and Muslims, became the spark which ignited the Sepoy rebellion. Before long, all disgruntle elements, high and low, joined the bandwagon in a bid to be rid of the unholy British power. The British call it a Sepoy mutiny but the universal nature of the uprising egged on by the disaffected Sepoys gave it the colour of an uprising at a level which can only be described as national.

While the main centres of rebellion were in Calcutta, Lucknow, Delhi, Meerut and Kanpur, reverberations were felt in Rajputana also. On 28 May 1857 the troops at Nasirabad cantonment near Masuda, joined the revolt. Capt. Spottiswoods and Col. Newbury were killed in the fracas. The troops plundered the bungalows, burnt records and left for Delhi. In August there was an outburst at the Ajmer Jail which was however quickly crushed. Akbar's lodge, now the Magazine, was fortified with reinforcements. In Marwar the Chief of the fiefdom of Auwa decapitated the Resident and hung his head on the main gate of the fortress. Auwa was ransacked by the British and reduced to rubble and the Jodhpur Durbar was asked to confiscate the Thikana. The Durbar complied though it was eventually restored to the family.

Every precaution was taken to see that similar incidents did not take place in the vicinity of Ajmer. Thus in July 1857 alarmed at hearing of the presence of a large force of Masuda cavalrymen at Nayanagar (Beawar) Capt. V. Priece, Second

Assistant to the Commissioner of Ajmer, was despatched to investigate forthwith. He writes: "On assuming charge of civil duties I found some 800 sawars (horsemen) of the Chief of Masuda employed in keeping open communications and patrolling the town of Nayanagar. They remained here for about three months and were (then) dismissed by order of Brig. General Lawrence". The 'dismissal' or disbanding of the Masuda cavalry arose out of rumours that in league with the Raja of Kishangarh there was a plan to divide the area Southwest and Northeast of Nasirabad between themselves in the event the British were forced to leave after the ongoing rebellion. The presence of the large cavalry at Beawar would have entitled Masuda to take back the Beawar area annexed by the British earlier, in such an eventuality. The dubious association of Sheonath Singh's predecessor Devi Singh with the Mers had precipitated the annexation of half the territory of Masuda in a thinly veiled exercise termed lease. No chances were being taken with his successor's cavalry.

After much bloodshed the rebellion was crushed by 1858 and the British reemerged supreme. The Mughal emperor was imprisoned, dethroned and exiled to Burma and the governance of India was transferred from the East India Company to the Crown, ending for good the surviving fiction of the Mughal Emperor and consigning the Mughals to history.

Unlike his predecessor, Sheonath was no Hercules. In an oil painting he emerges as a slender, sensitive poetic personality, cast in the image of his contemporary, Maharaja Ram Singh of Jaipur. He had the wisdom and capability to face the challenges of a new age. Despite the turbulence of the times he patronized poets and men of letters, showering them with gifts and rewards. His generosity towards poets became legendary and a burden on the treasury. He was also fond of moving incognito among poor peasants to enquire about their welfare and way of life and join in their rustic games. He was himself a poet and a compilation of Rajasthani poetry by him is still available in the Masuda archives.

He married twice. One Rani was Khangarotji from Dhundar near Jaipur and the other Sisodiniji from Banera in Mewar. Rajput wives do not adopt the clan names of their husbands but continue to be referred to by the names of the clans into which they were born. He died suddenly while on a vacation at a hill side palace in 1863. He had two daughters; one married at the principality of Kunadi in Kota and another to the Rajadhiraj of Shahpura but had no male issue.

The succession was decided by the British, favouring the closest preceding bloodline in the genealogical table in descent from Bhupati. No option was allowed to the Chief Rani to adopt a successor of her choice as in the past. Sheonath Singh's grandfather's brother Dev Singh's descendant was deemed to be the most legitimate option. Thus Bahadur Singh came to succeed to the Gaddi in 1863.

There are no miniature paintings available for the period after Devi Singh. Portraits of Sheonath Singh and Bahadur Singh are oil canvases by European artists. The art of miniature paintings had finally died out to be replaced by oil canvases and by the close of the nineteenth century by painted photographs.

# 13

# British Raj

## Bahadur Singh (1863 – 1904)

In his portraits and tinted photographs Bahadur Singh emerges as a portly, good natured and intelligent chief, sporting a bejeweled Mewari Pagri and beard and proudly displaying on his Angarkha tunic two impressive British decorations. Imperial Britain like their predecessor the Grand Mughals made it a point to liberally distribute a range of civil and military titles and decorations to the most deserving of their subjects at all levels of society from the aristocracy to the gentry and right down to ordinary members of the public. Bahadur Singh's decorations were in a class of their own. The Kaiser-i-Hind and the Commander of the Indian Empire medals, acknowledged his outstanding achievements, loyalty to the crown, administrative reforms and liberal education and beliefs. In later years he was styled as Rao Bahadur Singh KIH, CIE. Thus, like his predecessors who had won the approbation and trust of the Mughals, receiving Mansabs, honorifics, gifts, Sanads and insignia, he too joined the ranks of the most favoured aristocrats of the British Raj, succeeding thereby in reversing the impression of the duplicity of the previous two generations.

The British were now fully engaged in developing and modernizing Ajmer. In 1868 General Keating, Agent to the Governor General Rajputana, laid the foundation of the first modern educational institution, the Government College at Ajmer. Bahadur Singh lost no time in seeking to enrol at the college. In 1869 a Municipal Committee was established. Visits by other important officials were indicative of the purposeful development of Ajmer as a trend setter for Rajputana. General Cunningham D.G. of Archaeology and Sir D. Brandia I.G. of forests visited Ajmer and sent detailed reports and recommendations.

On 19 October 1870 the Viceroy and Governor General Lord Mayo made his celebrated visit to Ajmer and held a Durbar on 22 October at 9 AM in a grand complex of tents to receive all the Maharajas and the chiefs of Rajputana. The name of Rao Bahadur Singh is also sited among those of 41 Maharajas, Princes

**Bahadur Singh**

and Chiefs presented to the Viceroy. In addition to the Maharajas and Princes all other Ajmer Chiefs were also presented, including Bhinai, Sawar, Junia, Pisangan, Deolia, Para, Kharwa, Bandanwara, Govindgarh and Bagsuri. Also listed was the Dewan of the Ajmer Dargah. Most of the above or their descendants later studied at the Mayo College. At the ceremony all the Rajput nobility acknowledged the suzerainty of the British crown and offered 'Nazars', though the Maharana of Udaipur, in view of traditional and historical sensitivity was exempted from doing so. The Viceroy in response offered the Maharajas the traditional betel leaf and perfume, 'Pan and Attar', while his Foreign Secretary and Under Secretary did likewise to the other dignitaries, princes and chiefs. At the close of the ceremony they were conducted to their respective elephants, the limousines of yesteryear. Later the Viceroy paid return visits to the Princes and Chiefs.

A grand procession of elephants led by the Viceroy with the Princes and Chiefs in train passed through the city under a triumphal arch built with pillars of the famous 'Adhai-din-ka-Jhopra'. Ironically, it was Mohammed Ghori's Viceroy Qutub-ud-din Aibak who in 1199 had built this structure from the pillars of a ruined temple. Now the British Viceroy likewise cannibalized pillars from this structure to build a gateway through which his procession would pass. At night a grand illumination of the city was organized by Pandit Sheo Narayan for the Viceroy to witness from a ceremonial boat in the Ana Sagar Lake. Sheo Narayan later joined Mayo College as Head Pundit of its temple.

The idea had already been mooted by a Col. Walter in his Bharatpur Agency Report in 1869 that the sons of the aristocracy must be provided 'a liberal and enlightened education' and for this 'we must first of all establish an Eton in India', to ensure that the princes would promote 'peace, prosperity and progress amongst their own people'. The rebellion of 1857 made it imperative that the mind-set of the aristocracy needed to be developed methodically in favour of the new dispensation through a liberal education to avoid a repetition of such a threat to British rule. This recommendation therefore found immediate favour with the Viceroy.

At the Ajmer Durbar, Lord Mayo commenced his address by reassuring the gathered princess of Her Majesty's Government's desire "to secure to you and to your successors the full enjoyment of your ancient rights and assist you in upholding the dignity and maintaining the authority which you and your fathers have for centuries exercised in this land". This reassurance was doubtless made to assuage the concerns aroused by his predecessor, Lord Dalhousie's hated policy of lapse which had so fuelled the fire of rebellion. He also urged the rulers that "justice and order should prevail the length and breadth of Rajputana and every man's property be secure, travellers come and go in safety, cultivators enjoy the fruits of their labour and traders the produce of his commerce". He demanded that the rulers undertake construction of roads and irrigation works, encourage education and provide relief for the sick. Then having lectured them at length on the need for good governance he dwelt on his pet project – the establishment at

Mayo College Main Building

Ajmer of a school for educating the sons of Chiefs, Princes and Thakurs of Rajputana, "intended to make them fit for the important duties which in after life they would be called upon to discharge".

Herbert Sherring later Head Master of Mayo College writes in his book "The Mayo College – The Eton of India" published in 1897 that during his stay at Ajmer Lord Mayo also visited the boarding house for Ajmer Chiefs under the charge of Pandit Sheo Narayan. The Chiefs at the boarding house studied then at the Government College. Lord Mayo met the 13 students which Sherring mentions included first Rao Bahadur Singh of Masuda, his brother and eleven others. Among them were also two more scions of Masuda sub-fiefs, Sardul Singh of Sathana and Mor Singh of Jamola. In Sherrings words :

"Lord Mayo expressed great pleasure at what he saw and there is no doubt that in this small beginning he perceived the nucleus of what afterwards grew into Mayo College". It is evident that the aristocracy of Masuda was in the vanguard of the new wave to fully benefit from the educational opportunities that were now becoming available in Ajmer.

Responding to the Viceroys call with enthusiasm the Princes and chiefs contributed over Rupees 6 Laks for the purpose, matched by 6 Lakhs from the Government of India as endowment. Later the Maharajas built residential houses for each region and the British Government built a residence exclusively for the Ajmer Chiefs. The Government of India also built the main building in Indo-Saracenic style in solid marble. Sherring writes that it was a pity that the marble had not been polished and had it been "the Mayo College would rank next to the Taj Mahal in beauty of design and workmanship". The Maharaja of Jaipur had in fact offered to have the marble polished at his cost but the offer had not been accepted to keep the main building an exclusive contribution of the British and to prevent arousal of jealousies among the other princes. The project was completed in fifteen years. The opening ceremony of the school was performed by the Viceroy Lord Dufferin in 1885 and classes commenced soon thereafter.

Ajmer once again became a hub for development and progress in different fields which was then replicated in other parts of Rajputana. Maharajas and chiefs who gravitated to Ajmer to attend Durbars of Viceroys now also sent their wards and protégées to attend the new school for princes located there. The Mughal Suba of yesteryear had once again become a centre of attention and influence. It is noteworthy that the only students which Lord Mayo had met were from the Ajmer fiefs. Once again the Ajmer Chiefs found themselves in close proximity to the imperial power and they did not fail to grasp the advantage such opportunity offered.

Bahadur Singh's experiences at the Durbar, his meeting the Viceroy as a Chief but more personally as a student and listening to his progressive discourse made a lasting impression on him, spurring him to undertake administrative reforms and development activities in his fief. The first important reform he initiated was to abolish the prevalent system of farming out revenue to the trading classes, the Mahajans and money lenders in lieu of lump sum payments in advance. In its place he introduced the Kunta system of assessing rent and revenue directly from the farmer on the basis of classes of soil and produce assessed from field to field. House tax and tax on trade at Chowki-Chungis were also introduced to augment revenue. In place of the overbearing and all powerful Kamdars, he created Tehsils with officials assisted by resident police forces. The maintenance of Law and Order was also improved by creating 26 circles with Kiledars and Chawkidars assisted by horse and camel for patrolling. The 'Khazana' treasury was moved out from the Kamdar's residence where it had traditionally been located, to the Fort. The Chief Kamdar Kothari Vijayraj however continued to coordinate revenue collection and expenditure and retained his privileged position as senior most revenue official of the fief living in a palatial Haveli. At Masuda the central office was now called Huzur office with a Mir Munshi, the magistry and civil courts.

Bahadur Singh himself exercised the power of a first class magistrate with enthusiasm. With improved administration, law and order and the absence of marauders, brigands and invaders of the eighteenth century the fiefdom began to enjoy a period of peace, tranquility and growing prosperity, with clearly defined rights and duties of the citizens, security of property, trade and commerce. Such rights and duties were now justiciable in the courts with appeal resting at Ajmer.

Bahadur Singh also sought to do the Viceroy's biddings in undertaking irrigation projects. Three major anicuts were constructed round the town helping to raise the water level in the wells. Bundhs were built creating a tank named after him. During two famines he opened his granaries for the public, organizing kitchens for free distribution of food to the famine affected.

Bahadur Singh according to the customs of the times contracted five marriages. His marriage to the sister of the Maharana of Udaipur, Fateh Singh was the most prestigious. We see that the little fiefdom of Masuda which had always been wary of its great southern neighbour had now so grown in esteem and confidence as to be considered a fit suitor for the hand of the great Maharana's sister. The Maharana conferred the title of Rao on him which Lord Lytton the Viceroy formally recognized in 1877. All his successors continued to enjoy the title right to the present times.

It is a measure of Bahadur Singh's progressive thinking that he also became closely associated with the Hindu reformist movement of the renowned Swami Dayanand Saraswati, the founder of the Arya Samaj. His commitment to the movement was all the more remarkable for an aristocrat reared in the conservative atmosphere of orthodox and obscurantist ritual Hinduism, for the ideology of the reformist Arya Samaj condemned idolatry, pilgrimage, ritualism, the caste system, animal sacrifice, child marriage and dowry and called for equal rights for women including education. Swami Dayanand was also the first to speak of 'Swaraj' or India for Indians. Many regard him as the progenitor of the independence movement.

The Swami had met Bahadur Singh at Pushkar in 1878 and on his invitation the Swami spent a week with him that December. According to the chronicles of J.T.F. Jordens the Rao attended his lectures and "sealed their spontaneous friendship" by making a donation to the Arya Samaj. In 1881 during the Swami's visit to Ajmer he invited him for a longer stay at Masuda. Jordens adds "He was a guest of the prince for nearly two months at Masuda". Bahadur Singh during his visit arranged for debates and lectures conducted by the Swami, inviting Europeans and Jains and other heterogeneous groups. At a grand investiture ceremony amidst chanting of Vedic Mantras the holy thread was conferred alike on Brahmins, Kshatryas, Kayasths and Jains, in breach of orthodox caste norms. Jordens adds "the friendship with the Rao had become very close and the latter tried to persuade him to settle down in Masuda, promising to subsidize his movement". However the Swami after a long stay proceeded on his travels again. The Swami's movement had incensed orthodox Hindu sentiment. On his visit to Jodhpur Swami Dayanand Saraswati suddenly passed away. It is believed by many that he was poisoned. To this day one will find the portrait of Bahadur Singh prominently displayed in all Arya Samaj Temples of note and followers of the movement continue to enquire from his descendants about his life and times.

Towards the end of his rule, in recognition for his reforms, activities, loyalty, versatile career and progressive thinking he was conferred the prestigious order of Kaiser-I-Hind and in 1894 the ultimate distinction of Commander of the Indian Empire (CIE). The award is mentioned in the Pioneer of 6 February 1894; "The Chief Commissioner and A.G.G. Rajputana ... held a Durbar in the Kaiser Bagh for the purpose of delivering the badge and grant of C.I.E. to Rao Bahadur Singh of Masuda. He was supported by Mr. Martindale, Commissioner of Ajmer Merwara, Col. Prideaux, Resident of Oodeypore, Col. Abbot, Resident at Jodhpur etc. The grant was then read out by Capt. Melville and after the A.G.G. and C.C. had pinned the badge on the Rao's embroidered garment and shaken hands, the Rao read out his gratification".

Bahadur Singh's wives were Jhaliji of Gogunda (Mewar), Sisodiniji (Sister of Maharana Fateh Singh), Mansinghotji of Barwara (Jaipur), Ranawatji from Amla (Malwa) and Shekhawatji from Nawalgarh (Shekhawati). His only son, Sawai Ram Singh was born to the last Rani. He had two daughters, one married to the Rawat of Salumbar (Mewar) and the other, Rawal of Samod (Jaipur). Both remained issueless. His son was sent to study at Mayo College as was now customary. But the curse of the old lady of Sathana persisted in haunting the family and in its ultimate visitation, proved the most vengeful. While for two generations it merely denied the birth of an heir, in the third it cruelly devoured one already in existence. The young Sawai Ram Singh died of typhoid in his fourteenth year.

The doting father, at the height of his career and achievements, with every conceivable award and recognition to his credit, was suddenly bereft of his very

**Sawai Ram Singh**

raison d'etre. Bahadur Singh never recovered from the trauma of his irreparable loss and succumbed to his grief, dying inconsolable and devastated in 1905.

The people of Masuda sublimated their sorrow and sympathies in deifying Sawai Ram Singh. His commemorative pavilion in the family's ancestral enclosure is today a place of pilgrimage where it is said all wishes are granted. The merchants and traders of Masuda do not begin their day's work without first offering homage to the memory of the little prince at his shrine. Scores of others visit the pavilion offering coconut, incense and flowers and tie silken threads and scarves round the pillars in hope of their prayers being answered. The adoptive descendants of the House of Masuda visit the shrine on every visit to the town, particularly after a marriage in the family requiring the new bride or groom to pay him their respects. All members of the family maintain an altar in their homes with a photograph of the lad showing him standing in ankle long Angarkha and Pagri with arms akimbo.

Bijai Singh

# 14

# Last Days of British India

## Bijai Singh (1905 - 1938)

As Bahadur Singh died without a surviving male issue, once again the question of adoption reared its head. Every Thikana of the 'Bhayat's', the brotherhood in the dynastic tree descended from Bhupati, now felt it could have a legitimate claim to the succession. The fifth generation after Bhupati had spawned sub-fiefs for all the sons of Ajab Singh. Thus Sathana, Lamba, Nagar, Kesarpura, Lalawas, Sakrani and Jamola felt eligible to join the race as the generations at the base had all been exhausted in providing heirs. However there was a stronger claimant in the sixth generation from Bhupati. The descendants in the Thikana of Shergarh were closer to the base. There was yet one more claimant even closer in the ninth generation down at Nandwara, descended from Samrat Singh. It will be recalled that Jai Singh in the eighteenth century had nominated as heir, the son of his eldest son lost in battle, in preference over his surviving younger son Samrat Singh. The latter's mother had left for her parent's home the principality of Samod in Jaipur with her son in protest declaring prophetically that one day providence would right the injustice. That day for providential justice had now arrived a hundred and fifty years later.

A direct descendant of Samrat Singh. four generations later, was a boy of six in a remote branch of the Nandwara branch of the family tree at Sheopuri. The Sheopuri Thakur also had died providentially without issue. His brother Laxman Singh's surviving third son Nathu Singh succeeded to the Sheopuri Gaddi. Then again in the main branch of Nandwara the Thakur also died without issue and Nathu Singh being closest in line was adopted to Nandwara as well. When Bahadur Singh passed away without surviving issue, his candidature as the closest direct claimant became the most eligible for succession to the Gaddi of Masuda estate. But in the absence of any powerful elder to promote his claim and being a minor of six years, his candidature was brushed aside and forgotten.

The House of Shergarh felt that their claim was the most tenable and proceeded to occupy the Masuda Fort surrounding it with a force in the hope that the unchallenged fait accompli would be accepted by the British. Most centres of power and influence in the fief acquiesced to the Shergarh claim to being the heir presumptive. Yet there was one lone conscientious dissenter who decided to risk his life by apprising the British authorities at Ajmer of the developments and the full facts of the genealogical family tree. This humble personage was Pundit Nathulal Upadhyaya a mere teacher in the school at Masuda. In fact this namesake lived to tell the tale with pride time and again to Bijai Singh and his descendants, recounting his role in determining the succession, much as Coleridge's 'ancient mariner'. He sent a secret message with all due courage and despatch to the British at Ajmer. Promptly an armed force was sent under Col. Pencock, the siege lifted and the Shergarh contender despatched home.

The Colonel then held consultations with the Ranis but found their opinion ambiguous and divided. Till the matter could be thoroughly investigated and a decision taken, Mr. Erickshaw a Parsee official was appointed as administrator. The matter went up to the Privy Council at London and the process took a year and a half for a conclusion to be reached. Ultimately it was decided in favour of little Nathu Singh.

Thus the barefooted boy Nathu of Nandwara with his star on the ascendant and on the wings of a curse and a prophecy quickly climbed the third and ultimate rung in the adoption ladder, reaching its pinnacle as he was proclaimed the legitimate heir to the throne. A formal letter of recognition from the Viceroy through the A.G.G. was sent and read out in the open Durbar. A four horse carriage with erstwhile contenders humbly in attendance brought him to the fort for the investiture and the offerings of Nazrana by all the nobility and civilian order. However, destiny as is its wont, gave with one hand only to take with the other. He was separated from his natural family and placed in the care of the surviving Ranis who debarred his mother from ever meeting him again, lest his upbringing was prejudiced by rustic and inferior, undesirable maternal influences. To seal the metamorphosis from village lad to Rao, his very identity was changed and Nathu henceforth became known as Bijai Singh.

For fourteen years Masuda Raj remained under a Court of Wards during his minority. After Erickshaw, Mehta Purushottam Das a Gujarati was appointed as administrator by Government of India. It often happened that the administration under such Courts of Ward proved to be a blessing in disguise for the fiefs and states, with able administrators doing their best to bring about progressive reforms. At Masuda the administration was modernized and irrigation projects were undertaken, chief of which was the building of a Bandh named Bijai Sagar which helped to greatly increase the area under cultivation.

Meanwhile Bijai Singh was freed from the cloistered atmosphere of the fort and the Ranis and admitted to Mayo College as a boarder at Ajmer House on the campus. Bijai Singh was a conscientious and brilliant student and at the close of his academic career won the prestigious Sword of Honour for best all round student at Mayo College. There are photographs showing him as a handsome strapping youth in Khaki turban, jacket and Jodhpurs with high riding boots.

After leaving college he set about developing his estate. The fort was modernized and remodeled. Alas, in his zeal he tore down several Mahals with invaluable frescoes and paintings to be replaced by modern apartments. It is said that electricity came to Masuda Fort even before it had become common in Ajmer, through the installation of a Ruston generator. The fortress now appeared at night like a virtual Titanic, aglow with lights in the pitch black countryside. Visitors flocking to events and celebrations in the renovated fort were greeted by the barking of numerous pedigreed Labradors and Pomeranians. British games of strategy replaced chess and Chaupad. The modernized fort became a centre of social activity and partying with European guests and native gentry. Neighbouring chiefs gravitated to this splendid modern oasis in the wilderness.

His next venture was to set up a model farm with orchards of grapefruit, orange, grape, pomegranate and hybrid mango on a vast estate with a grand villa whose ceilings were painted with columns of fruits and flowers. A cattle farm was developed with superior breeds and hybrid cereals were sought to be grown. The farm became a model for good agricultural practices in the region. A tennis court and swimming pool were added for practicing sports learnt at Mayo College. The farm was named Bijainiwas but was known to the villagers as Model Farm.

He then embarked on his most ambitious project - the setting up of a township in Masuda territory near Bhilwara, as a hub for cotton ginning next to an existing railway line. The town was built in squares intersected by straight wide roads at right angles, doubtless inspired by Jai Sing's Jaipur. Entrepreneurs and industrialists were invited to set up mills, while he himself led the process by setting up his own ginning and processing factory. The railway line next to the town greatly enhanced its industrial and commercial potential in ginning, pressing and trading in cotton. The town came to be named after him as Bijainagar and is more prominently displayed on Indian maps today than Masuda itself which became eclipsed in size and importance.

He then undertook to start a transport agency which grew to be one of the largest networks in the region, raising the level of trade and commerce. He also set up several petrol pumps under his proprietorship in Ajmer.

In all this he was facilitated by two factors. Bahadur Singh had accumulated enormous wealth, given the stable regime under the Government of India, his modernization of revenue collection and reforms in irrigation and agriculture. But Bahadur Singh was extremely thrifty and given to hoarding gold ingots in his treasury. The young Bijay Singh, fresh from Mayo College felt that the hoarded wealth was most unproductive. His enterprises were therefore freely financed by the abundant gold in his treasury. Secondly, being born a man of the soil and not a conventional aristocrat he did not allow himself to be fettered by Kamdars and

Ajmer Chiefs with AGG. Bijai Singh seen second from left to AGG with ribbon and medal round neck

sycophants. He remained independent minded, pragmatic, dynamic and extraordinarily enterprising.

As his personal wealth grew from the agricultural, industrial and transport ventures he set about investing in real estate. After having modernized the Fort and built the palace on the farm and the factory complex he acquired for his residence at Ajmer a Nawab's palace which became a landmark in Ajmer by the name of Masuda House. Hitherto the Chiefs of Masuda resided in Haveli's in down town Ajmer, as was customary. Later he acquired a grand villa at Mussoorie, the hill station in the Himalayan foothills where the British and Indian elite and gentry congregated during summers visiting each other in rickshaws emblazoned with court of arms and pulled by liveried attendants. After his demise the property was acquired by the great industrialists of India the Birlas and today is Birla House.

His marriage to the princess of Danta state in Gujarat was an extravagant affair. A special train carried the thousand strong marriage party which was required by the generous hosts to enjoy his hospitality for weeks of festivity, for the unlikely reason that there was no auspicious date in the astrological almanac for them to leave before then. The marriage produced an heir, finally breaking the jinx of three preceding generations and one who survived into old age with abundant progeny of his own.

However his wife died a few years later of the scourge of the times, tuberculosis. He then married again, a niece of the Maharana of Udaipur, but this time he arrogantly insisted that contrary to custom the bridal party arrive at Masuda for the nuptials. She was prolific, giving him another six sons and two daughters. But this maverick star of the Mertia Jagmalot clan was short lived and died suddenly in his prime undergoing surgery at Mussoorie at the age of forty.

# 15

# Independent India

## Narayan Singh (1938 – 1992)

In traversing a thousand years, tracing the origins and history of the Mertia Jagmalots we have moved from a macrocosmic survey of Rajputs and Rathores to the microcosm of their chronicles. Inevitably as we come to the present times this survey appears to narrow down still further into the story of one family. It is as if zooming in on the Rajputs as planet earth we find that the blue globe transforms into an expanse of continents, the Rajput tribes and as our craft descends towards Terra Firma the outline of a single subcontinent, the Rathores, appears and before long a city turns into lanes and by-lanes of its family tree, till finally we observe a house with people, the present generation, and then one individual stands alone before us.

It has been an amazing journey through history, interwoven with individual careers. As we moved into the present, the lives of individuals became starker and more distinctive then the backdrop of history.

Narayan Singh succeeded Bijai Singh in 1938, a lad of nineteen. His life and times are particularly significant in our chronicles because they bring the Mertia Jagmalots into independent India, still in one piece. Evidently not only did they survive the storms and vicissitudes of history but once again employed their amazing skills, talents, capabilities and resilience to face the new challenges posed by an egalitarian, democratic India, which abolished their fiefdoms permanently. The feudal age which had both nurtured them and tested their metal had passed and a new dispensation now confronted them. They had adapted remarkably to the changing power structures which history threw up without succumbing, indeed profiting from every change. The ruthless invasions from the northern passes, the Sultans of Delhi, Gujarat and Malwa, the Mughals, the Marathas and the British had each posed a challenge to their capacity to survive and prosper, but their genius had made them emerge unscathed, more astute, empowered and prosperous. Many grand dynasties had withered and left without a trace, a prime example being the grand Mughals themselves but the Mertia Jagmalots emerged intact at independence.

This was not just another dispensation or change in command. Independence was a watershed with a complete reversal of the old order from the roots upwards. The transformation was total – political, intellectual, ethical, philosophical and systemic, confronting them with a challenge in adjustment beyond anything experienced so far.

Narayan Singh's life and times therefore assume unique importance. Having survived so far with distinction, how did they face the upheaval which their world now experienced? A survey of individual case histories, at the risk of recounting apparently tortuous and tedious details, becomes necessary to fathom whether the Mertia Jagmalots were up to their new challenge of history and whether they once again succeeded in emerging victorious, albeit on this occasion without sword or bloodshed.

Narayan Singh was the only child of Bijai Singh's deceased first Rani. He therefore confined his son since infancy to a separate loveless household full of guardians, instructors and keepers, restricting his interaction with his numerous lively siblings, out of concern for his security. Later while his siblings were educated at Mayo College, a school for princes, the patriarch, given his egalitarian bent and humble origins, sought to ensure that his eldest son and heir would not turn into another 'Bana' – an egotistical princeling with no other ambition in life than wine, woman and song. He was therefore packed off to the plebeian Government College Ajmer set up by the British to educate the commoner as a counterpoise to the aristocratic Mayo College. But there instead of shaping up as a proletarian, practical and down to earth son of the soil, the cordon of attendants thrown around him isolated him once again. This time from contact with the classes represented there. His brothers meanwhile mixed with members of the aristocracy and their own kind as equals and learnt the ways of the world without any fetters.

Narayan Singh therefore grew up to be an introverted, diffident individual, neither at ease with his aristocratic compatriots, nor intimate with the classes he encountered in the Government College. He never learnt to stand in a queue to buy a ticket or open a purse to pay for a purchase. However, his unconventional academic career and the stoic social environment did produce that rare aristocrat who was more interested in philosophical and intellectual pursuits than the proverbial wine, woman and song.

He proceeded for higher studies to the prestigious St. Stephens College and the renowned Allahabad University. There he was asked as a fresher standing alone and friendless in the corridors with a book in his hand by some senior students, bent on ragging, as to what he was reading. The shy Narayan Singh looked up and innocently said, the Bhagwad Gita to a roar of mocking laughter.

However, his academic career was cut short by the premature demise of his father and the call to assume responsibilities of the fiefdom and the care of his siblings and their mother. Several of his brothers were still in their infancy, his sisters were marriageable and other brothers required being educated further. He assumed these onerous responsibilities with conscientiousness and sobriety while still only nineteen. His stoic upbringing helped him to take on the burden without complaint. While others in his plight had been known to neglect and abandon their siblings, indulging in extravagant pursuits of pleasure and passions, Narayan Singh remained sensitive and anchored throughout his life to their concerns even above those of his own progeny, eventually finding the best matches for his sisters and educating his brothers both in India and overseas.

His marriage to Kamala, a beautiful princess of the fiefdom of Bissau in Jaipur state, provided the first spark of colour and joy in what so far had been a regimented and gloomy life. She weaned him away from unrequiting labour and responsibility, showing him that life could be fun. Bombay the metropolis of the East became a haven of escape.

Travel by Salon Class of the BB&CIE railways, American cinema, the company of Bolywood film stars, Bombay Race Course events, plush American eight seater limousines, shopping at the Army and Navy Stores, finest brocade saris, object d' art, jewellery at Gazdars, dances at the Taj Mahal Hotel, picnic parties and the company of sophisticated friends and aristocrats in the Bombay circuit replaced the cheerless and somber affairs of the estate, much to the alarm of the Kamdars back home. The handsome couple made heads turn wherever they went.

The Bombay frolics had been engendered by Kamala's association back home with the westernized Jaipur Durbar. It was customary for every noble in Jaipur to be given an Anglo-Saxon nickname by the Maharaja Sawai Man Singh. The heir, Bhawani Singh became 'Bubbles'. Her own brother Raghubir Singh of Bissau was usually known as 'George'. There were innumerable Henrys, Johns, Davids, Marys, Margarets and what have you, led by the fabled 'Ayesha' of Rider Haggard's best selling 'She' in its Indian incarnation of the legendary beauty, the third Maharani, Gayatri Devi and her polo playing husband. They were forever on jaunts to London and Europe accompanied by 'George', the Maharani's ADC.

The beauteous Kamala imbibed these influences first hand and herself became a head turning chiffon clad counterpart of her renowned mentor. She came to acquire no less than a hundred pairs of heels in brocades and satins, housed in great calf leather shoe cases. All the heirlooms in uncut emeralds and diamonds worn by Bahadur Singh at ceremonies were quickly and magically transformed by the great Gazdars of Bombay into fabulous necklaces and chokers which she sported. The Kamdars seeing the treasures vanish from the 'Khazana' warned of an old proverb that if a woman was ever allowed to enter the treasury, it would signal its disappearance. But Kamala could not be restrained or debarred and saw all.

The Masuda Rao and Rani now whisked through Bombay in an eight seater Oldsmobile with red velvet upholstery or alternatively a two tone Buick

Narayan and Kamala

Roadmaster. Soon an Art-Deco Warden Road type mansion was built upon a hilltop in Masuda replete with black and white Italian marble flooring and custom built teak furniture commissioned specially with the famed Kamdar group of furnishers. It now became the royal residence with the abandonment of the old Fort. Narayan Singh's contribution, given his artistic inclinations, was to fill the Mahal with the rarest object d'art from India and China. The couple now alternating between Bombay and base, organized duck shoots, antelope chases and hunts for Lords, Ladies and friends at Masuda. Tigers and panthers were shot and photographed with the proud hunters holding guns in the background of the fortresses, for posterity. While Narayan Singh joined these hunting sports he did so with a growing distaste for the mass killings of animals and birds.

Like Daphne du Maurier's 'Rebecca', Kamala impressed her persona on the new residence and was immortalized by the famous Bombay photographers Hamilton in life size colour portraits looking down from every nook and cranny of the Mahal and her 'K' monogram on every pillow case, stationary pad and crockery.

She gave birth in quick succession to a girl and two boys introducing Narayan Singh to the joys of family life for the first time in his formerly dreary life. But it was not long before this idyllic existence was rudely shattered. Kamala contracted Tuberculosis, incurable at the time. They then got embroiled with soothsayers, Swami's and rogue mystics who began to fleece them of their wealth with promises of miraculous cures which never came. The sudden switch to the occult stemmed from Narayan Singh's early mystical orientation and inclinations, which now asserted itself in crises with manic force. This case was not really as unique as it may appear. Rajput aristocracy was particularly prone to falling under the spell of unscrupulous Tantriks and charlatans when faced by insuperable adversity. General reliance on astrologers was always commonplace to determine every facet of life for rulers and ruled alike. The obsession rose to insane levels at critical moments in life when faith in the occult finally overcame reason.

The ailing Kamala having developed the unreasoning faith of the terminally sick was now persuaded to hand over her fabulous jewellery to appease the insatiable demands of the Tantriks, ostensibly for effecting an occult cure. These were no rustic Tantriks of Masuda but sophisticated swindlers of Bombay. The priceless jewels were conveniently condemned as evil and inauspicious and the very cause of her malady, to be rid of without delay. She was also persuaded to give up all allopathic medication at the behest of the Swamis, despite dire warnings from the best Doctors in the land, in exchange for holy ashes to be swallowed with honey and brandy. Thus she hastened her end on the eve of the discovery of streptomycin. The final months were horrific, ending in her tragic and painful death. By then, half the wealth of the estate in jewellery, silver and gold had been swindled away and the whole was only prevented from being lost by her early demise.

Narayan Singh with guests on a duck shoot.

Narayan Singh was now a crazed man after her funeral. Barely thirty at his bereavement and with three traumatized infants in train, the establishment decreed he remarry forthwith, someone who could be 'mother' to the kids. An appropriate lady of the right pedigree and disposition from Kherali in Saurashtra, Gujarat was selected for the widower, overruling his reluctance to entertain the idea. He was made to meet her in a restroom on a wayside railway station. His lack of a clear response was read as diffidence, the match was arranged and the marriage was solemnized soon thereafter.

Thus Shanti, renamed Urmila, came into his life. Aghast at the sorry state of affairs, but unable to voice the opinions of a new bride, she silently bore the continued ministrations of the diabolic mystics, who now promised to bring back the deceased to life, through further costly Tantric rituals that would surely have ruined the estate. The much younger but thoroughly practical Urmila then set about slowly but surely disabusing the mind of Narayan Singh and before long the mystics were sent packing after recovery of some of the silver on threat of police action.

Urmila restored Narayan to sanity. Coming from a conservative and traditional family unaffected by western culture she had no desire to be a Bombay socialite and was content to settle down back home in Rajasthan. Meanwhile Narayan Singh immersed himself in philosophical and scriptural studies, leaving the children in Bombay in the care of a guardian, governesses and staff to benefit from the good convent education available there.

With Urmila also came Indian Independence, ending both colonialism and feudalism and ushering in a new egalitarian, democratic order, a socialistic ethos and public antipathy towards the representatives of the old order. Narayan Singh adjusted quickly, relieved of the responsibility of his erstwhile fiefdom. The new leadership in token of the patriotism shown by the princely order in acceding to India with little resistance, allowed them retention of their personal property and titles and paid them sustenance in the shape of the Privy Purse, Compensation and privileges. This was no French Revolution with guillotines. It enabled India's 'ancien regime' to quickly adjust to and take advantage of the new circumstances. Narayan Singh entered politics and joined the Congress Party, readily discarding his double breasted 'Seville Row' suits, cuff links and tie pins and donning home spun Gandhian Khadi attire down to his underclothing, declaring his socialistic convictions. He ran for elections and easily won a seat in the Legislative Assembly from his erstwhile fiefdom, which had now become a constituency for the Rajasthan legislature. The Mer tribals of yore voted for him en bloc. He continued to win successive elections from Masuda constituency over several General Elections and first became Deputy Speaker and then successively Minister for Forests, Education etc.

He came to have a reputation for incorruptibility and selfless discharge of his duties and responsibilities. He took special care to develop his constituency, the erstwhile fiefdom, with far reaching projects in irrigation, education, health and

Narayan and Urmila Host Breakfast for PM Indira Gandhi,
Rajiv Gandhi and CM Sukhadia

administrative reforms. He also authored several books on the Upanishads, the Gita and one act plays on characters from the Puranas.

In his political life, Urmila became an active partner, offsetting his simplicity with her shrewd political acumen. She also engaged in social welfare activity in the constituency and elsewhere, seeking to ameliorate the plight of village women steeped in antiquated practices like 'Parda', providing them with skills and equipment to enhance their livelihood and make them less dependent. She rose to be Chairperson of Rajasthan Social Welfare Board and a confidante of the Prime Minister Indira Gandhi on local issues. Though barely educated herself she addressed large public gatherings with confidence and élan, calling upon women to rise and stand shoulder to shoulder with their men folk in all fields of endeavour. Narayan Singh and Urmila Devi were always placed by the Chief Ministers in the forefront for their charisma and sophistication during visits of the Prime Minister and overseas dignitaries. They also joined several delegations overseas representing India at parliamentary and social welfare fora.

On his passing away after a long and successful career the people of the constituency joined enthusiastically in paying him fitful homage, the likes of which were only accorded to the most dedicated leaders. At public demand a statue of Narayan Singh was commissioned and placed in the heart of the town. Thus Narayan Singh even after the abolition of the feudal order continued to be intimately involved with the affairs of his erstwhile fiefdom and helped develop it even more effectively than had his ancestors. Furthermore he made his signal contribution to regional and national affairs. This scion of the Mertia Jagmalots proved that despite a fundamental change in their fortunes in the twentieth century, they had once again with tact and ability fully adjusted to the circumstances and utilized all opportunities to remain at the top, while making their unique contribution to public life.

It would be interesting in our analysis to enquire how his siblings, the less fortunate Mertia Jagmalots fared. All his brothers were educated at Mayo College and proceeded thereafter to become graduates. Shambhu Singh the eldest son of Chavdiji his father's second Rani, became a Major in the Army. Jitendra, a Doctor of letters from Edinburgh, joined the Indian Institute of Public Administration as professor. Umaid joined the army and rose to the rank of Brigadier. Daulat settled in the USA and after a brief stint in Hollywood with Richard Burton and Lana Turner settled down as a professor at Syracuse University. Shiv Pratap migrated to the U.K, marrying an English lady and became a school teacher. Madhusudan remained at home with his mother taking care of her affairs. Incidentally, Chavdiji outlived Narayan Singh and most of her children save two, passing away only in her nineties. Sajjan married Devi Singh of Mandawa estate in Shekhawati and was enterprising in initiating a hand block printing business and starting a hotel at their fortress in Mandawa village, which today has grown to be a popular haunt on the world tourist map. Kaushalya married Raja Virendra Pratap Singh of Shohratgrh estate in U.P. helping him develop his extensive farms. We may note that they all became useful members of society in post Independent India making valuable contributions according to their inclinations and abilities. There were no dropouts.

The career of the next generation is even more important for an account about the acumen and abilities of the clan to continue the journey into the present times. The Prime Minister Mrs. Gandhi had moved a constitutional amendment to abolish Privy Purse, compensation payments and privileges of the princely order. This deprived them of any special status and now they were commoners competing on a level playing field with other Indians.

Narayan Singh and Kamala's eldest child Vijay Lakshmi married Sukhdev Singhji a scion of the Jadeja clan from Jamnagar in Gujarat, renowned for their prowess in the cricketing world. He began as an executive in the prestigious Burmah Shell and rose to be Chairman of Bharat Petroleum, doubtless with his Mertia Jagmalot wife's skills in housekeeping and socializing.

Narayan Singh's and Kamala's eldest son Indrajit Singh Rathore (the author) educated at Mayo College and St. Stephens College joined the Foreign Service through competitive examination and served as Consul General Sydney and as Ambassador of India to Madagascar, Comoros, U.A.E., Oman and Morocco, in a career spanning 38 years. He married his classmate, a double graduate, Amrita who proved an asset in his Foreign Service career. He being the eldest son of Narayan Singh succeeded as head of the family. The Mertia Jagmalot brotherhood joined at the investiture ceremony, together holding the long chord of the turban being tied on his head. Despite the abolition of all titles of the fiefdom, the brotherhood insisted on styling him as Rao Saheb. In post Independence India, among the erstwhile aristocracy it is now customary to continue to address one another with the defunct titles out of courtesy and a sense of history. Even outside the pale of the aristocratic order it is not uncommon for the general public and even people in authority to continue to address the princely order with their former honorifics.

Narayan Singh's second son Mohan Chandra Singh spent his life in true aristocratic style as a man of leisure. He married Pratibha, a princess of Katesar in the U.P.

Urmila's eldest son Amardeep remained at home looking after his estate. Her second son Dushyant became a hotelier and businessman, while her third son Durjai served in the Tea Estates before becoming a hotelier and a farmer.

A final word about Narayan Singh and Kamala's grandchildren would complete our chronicles and show how the Mertia Jagmalots continued their journey of survival into the 21$^{st}$ century.

Vijaylakshmi's son Kushalpal is a banker in Dubai. Her second son is in the Air Transport sector at Dubai Airport. Her daughter Anjali is also a banker in Mumbai.

Indrajit Singh Rathore's daughter Meera is a writer married to Kandarp Singh who has risen to be M.D. of Tetrapak in India, Bangladesh and Sri Lanka. Their son Dhruv is a student at the American School in New Delhi. Indrajit's son Parthsarthi Rathore, next in line for 'succession' as head of the dynastic order of Mertia Jagmalots, is a successful banker in New York, married to Sura of New York who is herself a banker.

Mohan Chandra Singh's sons Jagatdeep works for a consultancy firm and Shailendra is a manager at Reliance Refineries at Surat.

The youngest Mertia Jagmalot is Neel Rathore, son of Parthsarthi, resident of New York. This presumptive Rao of a glorious clan, in the generations to follow, reared in distant New York will doubtless one day get to read these annals of his forefathers and become acquainted with his extraordinary lineage and heritage.

This concludes the chronicles of the Mertia Jagmalots spanning a millennium. The story of many other clans in what was know as Rajputana would be identical, be they offshoots of the Sisodias, Rathores, Shekhawats, Chauhans, Kachwahas, Jadejas, Hadas or Bhatis.

# Epilogue

As one looks around one finds that the Mertia Jagmalots endured into the 21st century with many of the strengths and traits, customs and traditions of Rajput tribes wholly in tact. The qualities which James Tod extolled as venerable and heroic in his Annals have indeed survived into the present age. The Rajput is still many say, a cut apart, combining humility and pride, heritage and chivalry, discretion and etiquette, courage and sacrifice, diligence and determination, aesthetics and creativity, gravitas and charisma, grace and charm, patriotism and leadership.

In Independent India the Rajput has been Prime Minister, Vice President, Governor, Chief Minister, Justice, Ambassador, politician, diplomat, General, soldier, bureaucrat, entrepreneur, painter, writer, musician, covering every field of activity and making his valuable contribution to the nation.

Many are in politics where their potential is suitably employed. You find them in large numbers in the armed forces, on the front defending our borders and in the police force keeping the peace at home, something for which their martial skills make them particularly suited. Many have reinvented themselves as hoteliers by transforming their fortresses and palaces into hotels, thus enabling them to preserve, revive and promote the glorious traditions of their past in art, aesthetics, attire, cuisine and hospitality alluring wondering tourists from far and near to share and sample the grand cuisine and life styles of the past. In the academic field they have sought to preserve and develop the excellence and distinctive features of heritage Public Schools like Mayo College Ajmer, Rajkumar College Rajkot and Scindhia School Gwalior, reintroducing features like Polo and Golf in the curriculum to provide a comprehensive educational experience.

Their qualities are epitomized by an article of jewellery which Rajput ladies wear at ceremonial functions. This is a necklace or choker of enamel work on gold called Meena Kari; it looks beautiful and exquisitely crafted to the casual observer, but there is a twist. The fabulous enamel work for which the jewellery is renowned is not even visible, for it lies subtly hidden on the reverse as a mark of unique Rajput sophistication, sobriety and discretion. The Rajput is like that jewel, much more within, than what is visible on the surface.

The Rajput emerges as a quiet achiever who makes his contribution with dignity and circumspection and is today recognized as a valuable asset to the national weal, even as he was during the empires of the Mughals and the British and in history before the advent of Islamic Kingdoms. The peoples of the former fiefs would rather trust them with their future than an untried option and invariably vote them to their legislatures, which speaks volumes about the historical respect for the clans which had protected and provided for them through history's vicissitudes.

# Bibliography


Masuda Archives

Annals and Antiquities of Rajasthan - Lt. Col. James Tod (1829)

Chiefs and Leading Families in Rajputana - C.S. Bayley (1894)

The Mayo College, "The Eton of India" - Herbert Sherring (1897)

Tales from Indian History - Talboys Wheeler (1881)

Mediaeval India under Moham Medan Rule - Stanley Lane-Poole (1903)

Ajmer the Last Capital of the Hindu Empire - Harbilas Sarda (1923)

Life of Dayanand Sarasvati: World Teacher-Harbilas Sarda (1968)

Glories of Marwar and the Glorious Rathores- Pt. Bisheswar Nath Reu (1943)

New History of the Marathas - G.S. Sardesai (1948)

A History of the Maratha People - C.A. Kincaid & D.B. Parasnis (1931)

Emperors of the Peacock Throne - Abraham Eraly (1997)

# Index

## J



## K



## L



## M



## N



## O